Society of Biblical Literature
Monograph Series 16

Robert A. Kraft, Editor

Published for the
Society of Biblical Literature

Moses in Greco-Roman Paganism

John G. Gager

Abingdon Press

Nashville

New York

In the preparation of this study I have received guidance from numerous teachers and colleagues. I am especially indebted to Professor John Strugnell of Harvard University who advised me in producing the dissertation (1968) which underlies the present work.

JOHN G. GAGER

Contents

CONTENTS

Abbreviations

AJA	*American Journal of Archaeology*
AJP	*American Journal of Philology*
ArchP	*Archiv für Papyrusforschung*
ArchRW	*Archiv für Religionswissenschaft*
BA	*Biblical Archaeologist*
Bauer, *Lexicon*	*A Greek-English Lexicon of the New Testament and Other Early Christian Literature,* compiled by W. Bauer and translated by W. F. Gingrich and F. W. Arndt, 1957
CIJ	*Corpus Inscriptionum Judaicarum,* ed. J.-B. Frey, 2 vols., 1936-1952
CPJ	*Corpus Papyrorum Judaicarum,* ed. V. Tcherikover, A. Fuks and M. Stern, 3 vols., 1957-1964
CQ	*Classical Quarterly*
CR	*Classical Review*
DJD	*Discoveries in the Judaean Desert*
ET	English translation
Festugière, *Révélation*	A.-J. Festugière, *La révélation d'Hermès Trismégiste,* 4 vols., 1950-1954

FGH	See Jacoby, below
Fr.	Fragment
Goodenough, *Symbols*	E. R. Goodenough, *Jewish Symbols in the Greco-Roman Period,* 13 vols., 1953-1968
HN	*Historia Naturalis,* Pliny the Elder
HTR	*Harvard Theological Review*
Jacoby, FGH	F. Jacoby, *Die Fragmente der griechischen Historiker,* 15 vols., 1923-1958. References to fragments in Jacoby's collection are given according to the number assigned to the respective author and the number of the particular fragment (e.g., FGH 264, Fr. 6). Jacoby's comments are referred to by volume and page (e.g., FGH 3a:283)
JBL	*Journal of Biblical Literature*
JNES	*Journal of Near Eastern Studies*
JQR	*Jewish Quarterly Review*
JR	*Journal of Religion*
JRAS	*Journal of the Royal Asiatic Society*
JRS	*Journal of Roman Studies*
JTS	*Journal of Theological Studies*
LCL	*Loeb Classical Library*
Lewis-Short	*A Latin Dictionary,* ed. C. T. Lewis and C. Short, 1879
Liddell-Scott-Jones	*A Greek-English Lexicon,* compiled by H. G. Liddell *et al.,* 9th ed., 1940 (with a supplement by J. Barber *et al.,* 1968)
LXX	Septuagint
MGWJ	*Monatsschrift für Geschichte und Wissenschaft des Judentums*
MT	Masoretic text
P	Papyrus
PG	Migne, *Patrologia Graeca*
PGM	*Papyri Magicae Graecae,* ed. and tr. K. Preisendanz *et al.,* 2 vols., 1928-1931
RAC	*Reallexicon für Antike und Christentum,* ed. Th. Klauser *et al.,* 1950-
RBibl	*Revue Biblique*

RE	*Paulys Realencyclopädie der klassischen Altertumswissenschaft,* ed. G. Wissowa *et al.* References are to the number of each half-volume and its date
REJ	*Revue des Études Juives*
RHPR	*Revue d'Histoire et de Philosophie Religieuses*
RHR	*Revue de l'Histoire des Religions*
Schürer	E. Schürer, *Geschichte des jüdischen Volkes im Zeitalter Jesu Christi,* 4 vols., 3-4th ed., 1901-1911; repr. 1964. See also ET of older ed. in 5 vols., 1890 f.; abridged ed. by N. N. Glatzer, 1961
TAPA	*Transactions of the American Philological Association*
TDNT	*Theological Dictionary of the New Testament,* ed. G. Kittel *et al.* and tr. G. W. Bromiley. Grand Rapids: Eerdmans, 1964-
ZNW	*Zeitschrift für die neutestamentliche Wissenschaft und die Kunde der älteren Kirche*
ZTK	*Zeitschrift für Theologie und Kirche*

Introduction

*I intend to write the life of Moses, whom
some call the lawgiver of the Jews. . . . For
while the fame of his laws has spread throughout the world and reached the ends of the
earth, not many know him as he really was.
Greek authors have not wanted to record
him as worthy of memory, in part out of envy
and also because in many cases the ordinances
of local lawgivers are opposed to his.*

Philo, *Mos.* 1.1 f.

The intention of this study is to examine the figure of Moses—his life,
his person, and his teaching—as recorded by pagan authors in the
Greco-Roman world. What did they know, or claim to know, of
him? What did they think of him, and what factors (social, political,
literary, etc.) influenced their evaluation of him? Where did they
get their information? Was there anything like a fixed image, or
images, of Moses? To my knowledge there exist only two treatments

15

of the subject in modern literature: an article by I. Heinemann[1] on Moses in selected pagan and Jewish authors, and an article by E. Norden[2] which deals exclusively with Poseidonius and his supposed influence on later writers. While both treatments have proved helpful in my own work, neither has done full justice to the breadth and diversity of material to be found in pagan writings.

Perhaps a word should be said about the decision to focus exclusively on pagan authors. Earlier scholarship has devoted considerable attention to the image of Moses in Jewish and Christian writings.[3] The present study will make use of such material where it is revelant to pagan discussions of Moses. As for the Christian writings, the image of Moses is largely independent of pagan traditions. Although Christian writers did not hesitate to adopt pagan criticisms of the Jews as a people,[4] they seem not to have adopted pagan attitudes toward Moses. The reason for this is at least twofold. As one might expect, Christian authors derived their information about Moses directly

[1] "Moses," RE 16 (1935) : 359-75.

[2] "Jahve und Moses in hellenistischer Theologie," *Festgabe für A. von Harnack* (1921) , pp. 292-301.

[3] H. Cazelles *et al., Moïse, l'homme de l'alliance* (1955), has sections on the Old Testament, Judaism, the New Testament, the Christian tradition (Syria, Gregory of Nyssa, the Latin fathers) , liturgy and iconography, and Islam; H. Teeple, *The Mosaic Eschatological Prophet* (JBL Monograph Series 10, 1957), deals with Jewish and early Christian literature. J. Daniélou, *From Shadows to Reality* (ET 1960) includes a chapter (pp. 153-226) on typological uses of Moses and the exodus in early Christian writings; J. Jeremias, "Μωυσῆς" TDNT 4 (1967) : 848-73, covers Jewish as well as Christian material; and W. A. Meeks, *The Prophet-King: Moses Traditions and the Johannine Christology* (1967), includes chapters on Moses in the writings of Philo, Josephus, Qumran, the rabbis, the Samaritans, and the Mandaeans.

[4] See the long list of Christian anti-Jewish themes, together with their pagan counterparts, in J. Juster, *Les juifs dans l'empire romain*, 1 (1914) , p. 45 n. 1. On the general subject of the Jews in pagan literature, see M. Radin, *The Jews Among the Greeks and Romans* (1915) ; I. Heinemann, "Antisemitismus," RE Suppl. 5 (1931) : 3-43, and "The Attitude of the Ancient World Toward Judaism," *Review of Religion* 4 (1940) : 385-400; J. Leipoldt, *Antisemitismus in der alten Welt* (1933) and "Antisemitismus," RAC 1 (1950) : 469-76; R. Marcus, "Antisemitism in the Hellenistic-Roman World," in *Essays on Antisemitism* (1946) , ed. K. Pinson, pp. 61-78; R. Wilde, *The Treatment of the Jews in the Greek Christian Writers of the First Three Centuries* (1949), esp. pp. 32-77; V. Tcherikover, *Hellenistic Civilization and the Jews* (ET 1959) , esp. pp. 357 ff.; L. Feldman, "Philo-Semitism Among the Ancient Intellectuals," *Tradition* 1 (1958/59) : 27-39; and most recently *Bibliographie zur jüdisch-hellenistischen und intertestamentarischen Literatur: 1900-1965* (Texte und Untersuchungen 106, 1969) , ed. G. Delling, esp. the literature cited on pp. 30-32.

from Jewish sources rather than indirectly from pagan authors. A more important factor, however, was the direct historical and religious link between Judaism and Christianity. Both struggled over the "exclusive rights" to the possession and interpretation of the Jewish scriptures and their history. Both claimed the heritage of Israel as their own, and for this reason they often differed fundamentally in their attitude toward Moses. Lysimachus and Quintilian, for example, could reject Moses altogether, whereas Paul (Rom. 10:19) and Tertullian (*An Answer to the Jews*, 1-6, 10), while rejecting the validity of the Mosaic law after the coming of the Messiah, still accepted Moses as an important figure in the plan of salvation which they, as Christians, regarded as their exclusive inheritance. No pagan writer could or did affirm this much of Moses.

As concerns the method of approach to the subject, I have divided the material into four main chapters. In the first three chapters I have dealt with authors and texts[5] in chronological order; the fourth chapter is arranged topically. Chapter one deals with Moses as a wise lawgiver who established Jewish civilization on the foundations of ancient philosophical and religious traditions. Moses' reputation as a wise man was strong enough so that some writers could cite him as an authority in support of their own philosophical and religious belief. Chapter two focuses on negative attitudes toward Moses the lawgiver. To a large extent, criticism of Moses centered in Rome. This is not surprising in view of the political and religious conflicts between Rome and the Jews from the time of Pompey to the destruction of the temple in 70 c.e. A second phase in pagan criticism of Moses came after *ca.* 150 c.e., when Christianity began to occupy the attention of the pagan world. At this point, criticism of Moses became part of attacks on the Christians. One result of this new phase was that Moses' earlier reputation recovered considerably as he was favorably contrasted with Jesus and the Christians. Chapter three concerns the second main center of conflict between pagan culture and the Jews, i.e., Alexandria. Here the hostility of Greco-Egyptian civilization expressed itself in anti-Jewish accounts of the exodus. Moses was portrayed as a renegade Egyptian priest who turned against his former

---

[5] As a general rule I have included the Greek and Latin texts only where they do not appear in the collection of Th. Reinach, *Textes d'auteurs grecs et romains relatifs au judaisme* (1895; repr. 1963), or where they are otherwise not readily available.

17

religion and counseled his followers, a group of unclean Egyptian exiles, to despise everything foreign and to destroy temples wherever they found them. Similar accounts also appeared outside Egypt where they were used to explain the origins of the Jews. Chapter four moves from the literary to the world of magic and alchemy. Here Moses enjoyed considerable renown. His contest with the magicians of Pharaoh (Exod. 7:11 f.) is reported with varying degrees of inaccuracy. His name appears frequently in the magical and alchemical papyri both as the recipient of special divine wisdom and as the author of books and individual recipes. His name also appears on several amulets and phylacteries.

Obviously, such a study of Moses in Greek and Roman authors cannot avoid touching the problem of ancient anti-Semitism. In a sense I have regarded this project from the beginning as a case study in the origins of western anti-Semitism. It is my hope that it will contribute to the elucidation of this difficult subject by isolating one of its components, namely the figure of Moses, rather than trying to encompass the entire field. In contrast to an earlier stage of scholarship, recent studies have emphasized the diversity and complexity of attitudes toward the Jews in classical antiquity. In a recent work on the history of anti-Semitism, E. H. Flannery makes two comments which the reader of the present work should keep in mind:

> The true anti-Semites of the Roman Empire were neither the emperors nor the people, but the intelligentsia. Ancient pagan anti-semitism . . . is neither 'eternal' nor the constant companion of Jewish existence.[6]

Our study of Moses clearly confirms the observation that anti-Semitism was not a constant companion of the Jews in antiquity, but it should also demonstrate that there was even a greater range of views precisely among the intelligentsia than Flannery would lead us to believe.

The Life of Moses

Moses was by far the best-known figure of Jewish history in the pagan world. Of his life, however, little was recorded, and even this

[6] *The Anguish of the Jews* (1965), pp. 19 and 23.

18

little shows that the information was derived mostly from non-biblical sources.

Concerning his origins there were two opinions, one that he was a native Egyptian, the other that he was of Jewish descent. The theory of Egyptian descent appears primarily in the Alexandrian anti-Jewish writers of the first centuries B.C.E. and C.E.[7] In the accounts of Pseudo-Manetho, Chaeremon, Apion, and perhaps even Tacitus, Moses appears as a native Egyptian priest who was expelled from Egypt along with a group of polluted inhabitants (see below, pp. 113 ff.). According to Chaeremon, Moses' Egyptian name was Tisithen, according to Ps-Manetho, Osarsiph. Related to this strongly anti-Jewish version of Moses' origin, but quite different in tone, is the rather friendly report of Strabo, where Moses is described as "one of the priests . . . from lower Egypt" who left the country because of his disaffection with Egyptian animal worship (see below, pp. 38 ff.).

The tradition of Moses' Jewish descent appears in Apollonius Molon and Pompeius Trogus. The former presents a somewhat confused genealogy of Moses: "Gelos [sc. Isaac] had eleven sons by a woman of the country and a twelfth by the name of Joseph; from him the third was Moses."[8] Th. Reinach[9] and E. H. Gifford[10] interpret the final phrase (apo toude triton) to mean the third generation from Joseph, i.e., his grandson, while Heinemann, on the basis of the parallel between "third" and "twelfth," translated "his third son was Moses."[11] Perhaps it is not possible to choose between the two alternatives, but

[7] In passing one should note that the name Moses is quite possibly of Egyptian origin; see J. G. Griffiths, "The Egyptian Derivation of the Name Moses," JNES 12 (1953) : 225-31.

[8] Eusebius, Praep. Evang. 9.19.3 (421a). In the preceding sentence Apollonius says that Abraham's son by his Greek wife was called Laughter, Gelōs. The same etymology appears in Philo, Leg. All. 1.82. The name in Hebrew (Yizḥaq) is related to the term for laughter; cf. Gen. 17:17—"Abraham fell on his face and laughed (wayyizḥaq), and said, "Shall a child (Isaac) be born . . . ?" Similarly, in the preceding paragraph (420d) Apollonius interprets Abraham's name to mean "Father's Friend." Here the etymology is based on raḥam ("love"). In both cases Apollonius must have derived his information from a Jewish source; on Apollonius, see below, pp. 119 f. On Philo's use of name etymology, see E. Stein, Philo und der Midrasch (Zeitschrift für die alttestamentliche Wissenschaft, Beiheft 57, 1931).

[9] Textes, p. 61.

[10] Ed. and ET, Eusebii Praeparatio Evangelica, 3.2 (1903) : 452.

[11] "Moses," p. 362. For this possibility there is an interesting parallel in Pompeius Trogus, who makes Moses Joseph's son and in turn Aaron's father, diverging from the biblical genealogy on both counts. On Pompeius, see below, pp. 48 ff.

19

in either case Apollonius or his source has given a garbled version of the biblical genealogy. For it was Jacob, not Isaac, who had the twelve sons, and Moses was not the son of either Joseph or Isaac but of Amram, a descendent of Levi (1 Chron. 6) .[12]

Even the name of Moses was subject to misconstruction. According to the Suidas notice on Alexander Polyhistor, the first-century B.C.E. author of a writing *On the Jews*, the name became Moso (feminine) : "He also wrote . . . five books on Rome. In them he says that there lived a Hebrew woman by the name of Moso who wrote the law code of the Hebrews." [13] This mention of Moso has prompted considerable speculation. Some have denied the accuracy of the report on the basis that such a gross error cannot be reconciled with Polyhistor's otherwise considerable knowledge of the Jewish scriptures. Th. Reinach[14] has proposed that Polyhistor actually intended to designate the authoress of the Jewish *Sibylline Oracles*. Heinemann describes the tradition as malevolent and calls attention to similarly ill-intentioned transformations of male names: Cleomene for Cleomenes in Aristophanes *Nubes* 680, and Chrysippa for Chrysippus in Cicero *De Natura Deorum* 1.93. Finally, F. Jacoby discards all these explanations and declares the whole problem insoluble.[15] This much can be said: If Suidas' notice is correct and if Polyhistor recorded it in good faith, it represents but one of many bits of misinformation about Moses in pagan literature.

Of Moses' education and childhood, popular themes in Philo and Josephus, nothing is said. Interest, or perhaps available information, centered on his adult life. Even here only three, possibly four, particular events achieved recognition—his contest with the court magicians of Pharaoh, the exodus, the giving of the law, and perhaps his campaign against the Ethiopians. The last-mentioned is somewhat doubtful. B. Z. Wacholder has proposed Nicolaus of Damascus as the

---

[12] Other errors appear in the preceding paragraph 9.19.2 (420d) where Apollonius makes Abraham the third generation after Noah, whereas Gen. 11 counts eleven, and 9.19.2 (421a) where Abraham is confused with his son Ishmael.

[13] Suidas *s.v. "Alexandros ho Milēsios."* On Polyhistor, see J. Freudenthal, *Hellenistische Studien 1-2: Alexander Polyhistor* (1875), pp. 16-35; Schürer, 3: 469-72. His work *On the Jews*, to which we owe practically all our knowledge of pre-Philonic Hellenistic Jewish literature, is preserved in Eusebius' *Praeparatio Evangelica*.

[14] *Textes*, p. 65, n. 2.

[15] Heinemann, "Moses," p. 360; Jacoby, FGH 3a:283.

20

source for the Jewish story of Moses' military expedition against the Ethiopians at the head of the Egyptian army.[16] An extended version of the story appears in Josephus (*AJ* 2.238-53), while an earlier and much shorter version is recorded by Artapanus.[17] Wacholder attributes the expanded version of the story to Nicolaus. In Josephus, the story narrates the invasion of Egypt by the Ethiopians and the request of the Egyptian king, on advice of an oracle, that Moses assume leadership of the Egyptian forces. By a clever military maneuver he caught the Ethiopians off guard and drove them into their strongly fortified city. But he succeeded in taking the city only when the daughter of the Ethiopian king, entranced by his military prowess, proposed marriage to him in return for which he demanded the surrender of the city. Wacholder's argument that the "prominent role of women, the Egyptian conspiracy against Moses and the anti-Egyptian bias . . . strengthen the suspicion that we have here Nicolaus' version of the story" is not convincing.[18] The much shorter version of Artapanus is a purely Jewish creation, and its subsequent embellishment shows no traces of non-Jewish influence. Thus there is good reason to believe that the story probably circulated in the Alexandrian Jewish community and eventually made its way to Josephus through Jewish channels.

The story of Moses' and Aaron's contest with the magicians of Pharaoh (Exod. 7:10-12) shows up in several authors, Numenius of Apamea records a version in which the Egyptians, nameless in Exodus but called Jannes and Jambres/Mambres in later Jewish and Christian tradition, succeed in turning away the plagues which Moses calls down on the land (see below, pp. 139 f.) . Before Numenius, Pliny the Elder and Apuleius had mentioned a magical sect which claimed descent from Moses and Jannes (see below, pp. 137 ff.) . This garbled shred of information indicates that their knowledge of the story was at best secondhand and that they probably knew nothing more than the names of the characters.

Two events of Moses' career form the core of practically every pagan account of Moses—his leadership of the exodus from Egypt and his status as the lawgiver of the Jews. From Hecataeus of Abdera, the

---

[16] *Nicolaus of Damascus* (1962) , pp. 57 f.
[17] *Apud* Eusebius, *Praep. Evang.* 9.27.6 f. (432cd) ,
[18] *Nicolaus,* p. 58.

first Greek writer to mention Moses, to the Emperor Julian some six hundred years later, these two elements form the foci around which pagan authors painted their pictures, sometimes friendly, sometimes hostile, of Moses. Thus the bulk of our study will concentrate on Moses as the leader of the exodus and as the lawgiver of the Jews.

Appropriately, the final event of Moses' life to be recorded in pagan literature is his death. In the *Historia Augusta,* the author of the *Vita Claudii* laments the brief reign of M. Aurelius Claudius Augustus (268-270). In this connection he discusses the normal term of life and cites an anecdote about the death of Moses to illustrate his point that any kind of death would have been premature and inappropriate for Claudius:

> The most learned astrologers have asserted that one hundred and twenty years have been given man for living and that no one has been granted more; but they add that Moses alone, the friend of god as he is called in the books of the Jews, lived one hundred and twenty-five years; when he complained that he was dying young, it is said that an answer was given him by an unknown deity[19] that no one would live longer. But even if Claudius had lived for one hundred and twenty-five years . . . (25.2.4-5).

It is obvious from this paragraph alone that the author of the *Vita* possessed some knowledge of Judaism. The reference to Moses' designation as *familiaris dei* in Jewish writings recalls Philo who frequently calls him "friend of god" (e.g., *Mos.* 1.156) and especially the Jewish *Sibylline Oracles* where Moses is described as "the great friend of the most high" (2.245).

If on the other hand, "the books of the Jews" refers to the Jewish scriptures, the obvious reference would be to Exod. 33:11 ("Thus the Lord used to speak to Moses face to face, as a man speaks to his friend"). The figure of one hundred and twenty-five years raises several problems. It contradicts both biblical and later Jewish tradi-

---

[19] For the use of the phrase *incertum numen,* see the statement in Lydus *Mens.* 4.53, that Lucan described the god of the Jerusalem temple as *adēlos theos.* See the discussion by W. Schmid, "Bildloser Kult und christliche Intoleranz," in *Mullus* (Festschrift Th. Klauser, 1964), pp. 304-6. Schmid argues convincingly, on the basis of Lydus' statement, that *numen incertum* in the *Vita Claudii* is an almost exact equivalent of Lydus' phrase, and thus a precise designation of the god of the Jews; Lucan's use of the phrase *incertus deus* in his *Bellum Civile* (2.592 f.) makes this all but certain: *dedita sacris/incerti Iudaea dei.*

tions which are unanimous in giving the age of Moses at his death as one hundred and twenty. More seriously, at least from a pagan perspective, it elevates Moses above even Claudius by making him the single exception to the normal limit of one hundred and twenty years. Thus, unless the text itself is corrupt, the author bestows on Moses the honor of having lived longer than any other man.[20]

For Moses' unwillingness to die, there is an interesting parallel in the rabbinic midrash, *Petirat Mosheh* ("Death of Moses").[21] When told by a mysterious voice that the day of his death had arrived, Moses implored the Holy One, his angels, even heaven and earth, to delay the fateful hour and to allow him at least a glimpse of the promised land; naturally the Holy One refused to change the day or even the hour of his decree, but he did grant Moses a vision of the land, and at Moses' death descended himself to receive Moses' soul and to assume personal responsibility for his obsequies. However he came upon the story, the Roman author obviously knew a tale of Moses' death in a form related to the *Petirat Mosheh*. He may have known a good deal more about Moses than this anecdote, and the manner in which he introduces Moses' name without explanation indicates that he expected his readers to recognize at least the name and perhaps more.

To judge by the literary evidence alone, most pagan authors seem to have known just the bare outlines of the life of Moses. Only Numenius and the author of the *Vita Claudii* show familiarity with events other than those surrounding the exodus and the giving of the law, and in both cases their information comes from extra-biblical traditions. Other notable exceptions are Alexander Polyhistor in the pre-Christian period, and Celsus, Numenius, Porphyry, and Julian in the later centuries. The former, through special personal circum-

[20] For a different view of the passage, see R. Syme, "Ipse Ille Patriarcha," in *Historia-Augusta-Colloquium: 1966/67* (1968), p. 127 (repr. in Syme, *Emperors and Biography: Studies in the Historia Augusta* [1971], pp. 17-29). Syme regards the figure as the result of a playful tinkering and nothing more.

[21] See M. Abraham, *Légendes juives apocryphes sur la vie de Moïse* (1925), pp. 28-45 (introduction and bibliography), and pp. 93-113 (translation). The date of the midrash is uncertain, but Abraham places its present form no later than the seventh century c.e. The fact that the same motif occurs in the targum of Ps-Jonathan to Deut. 32 indicates that the tradition is considerably earlier than the date of the midrash itself. On Moses' refusal to die, see L. Ginzberg, *Legends of the Jews*, 5:77; 6:46 and 161.

stances, and the latter, through the knowledge of the Jewish scriptures brought about by the expansion of Christianity, knew the biblical story of Moses at first hand. To a considerable extent, this direct knowledge of the Jewish scriptures explains the differences between the figure of Moses in pagan authors who wrote before *ca.* 150 c.e. and those who wrote thereafter.

1. Moses the Wise Lawgiver of the Jews

First and foremost, the pagan world knew Moses as the lawgiver of
the Jews. The Greeks had a term for this; they called him *nomothetēs*.
Roman authors, on the other hand, failed to use or develop a convenient equivalent for *nomothetēs*. The term *legifer* does occur, but only
in Christian authors;[1] *legislator* and *legumlator* were available but
were not applied to Moses.[2] Instead Roman authors described his
activities according to their own opinions of him and the information
at hand. The least hostile of these authors, Pompeius Trogus, calls him
"leader of the exiles." Others, like Tacitus and Juvenal, simply
portray his legislation as contrary to acceptable Roman norms, while
Quintilian, who does not mention his name at all, classifies him among
those "founders of cities" who are a scourge to other nations and
refers to him as the "creator of the Jewish superstition." The simple
fact of diction reveals something of underlying attitudes. *Nomothetēs*
in Greek and *legislator* in Latin were terms of respect, reserved for
honored figures of the hoary past. The different fate which Moses

---

[1] According to Lewis-Short, *s.v. legifer:* Lactantius, *Div. Inst.* 4.17.7; Tertullian,
Apol. 19.4; Prudentius, *Perist.* 3.363. In Isa. 33:22 it is used of God.

[2] In the Vulgate, *legislator* is used twice of God (Job 36:22; Jas. 4:12) .

25

underwent in the two cultures is to some extent reflected in the application of these terms to him.

Hecataeus of Abdera

The earliest reference to Moses in pagan Greek literature occurs in the *Aegyptiaca* of Hecataeus of Abdera[3] who wrote his work during the early reign of Ptolemy I.[4] Unfortunately the original work of Hecataeus has entirely disappeared, and except for a few brief references to the *Aegyptiaca* in later writers,[5] the only extensive fragment or quotation is preserved in the *Bibliotheca* of Photius[6] which is in turn an excerpt from Diodorus Siculus:[7]

(1) As we are about to give an account of the war (of Pompey) against the Jews, we have thought it fitting to survey the origins of this people as well as their customs.

When a serious pestilence arose in ancient Egypt, the populace attributed the cause of the difficulties to the divinity. Inasmuch as many different groups of foreign aliens were living there and following foreign practises with respect to the temple and sacrifices, the result was that the traditional worship of the gods had been neglected. (2) Thus the natives supposed that unless they removed the foreigners there would be no end of their difficulties. After the foreigners had been banished, the most outstanding and active of them banded together and were cast, as some say, into Greece and certain

[3] There are two possible candidates who might claim to have preceded Hecataeus. According to Ps-Justin, *Cohortatio ad Gentiles* 10A, the Greek historians Hellanicus (b. *ca.* 500 B.C.E.) and Philochorus (d. *ca.* 260 B.C.E.) made mention of Moses in their chronicles of early Attica: "They [i.e., Hellanicus, Philochorus, Cadmus, Thallus, and Alexander Polyhistor] mentioned Moses as a most ancient and distant leader of the Jews." Had Hellanicus and Philochorus actually mentioned Moses, we can assume that Jewish and Christian apologists would have made use of them. Josephus is familiar with Hellanicus (*Ap.* 1.16) but knows nothing of a reference to Moses; so also Clement of Alexanderia (*Strom.* 1.[15.] 72.2).

[4] So W. Jaeger, "Der älteste griechische Bericht über die Juden," in *Diokles von Karystos* (1938), pp. 134-53, and Jaeger, "Greeks and Jews: The First Greek Records of Jewish Religion and Civilization," *JR* 18 (1938) : 127-43. For the meager details concerning Hecataeus' life and writings, see FGH 264 and 3a:31 f. Cf. also O. Murray, "Hecataeus of Abdera and Pharaonic Kingship," *Journal of Egyptian Archaeology* 56 (1970) : 141-71.

[5] Diod. Sic. 1.46.8; Diog. Laert. 1.9 ff.; Plut., *De Is. et Os.* 354 C-D.

[6] *Photii Bibliotheca* 244, ed. I. Bekker (1824), col. 380a. 7 ff. On Photius, see K. Ziegler, "Photios," RE 39 (1941) : 667-737, and F. Dvornik, *The Patriarch Photius in the Light of Recent Research* (1958).

[7] Designated as 40.3 in vol. 5, *Diodori Bibliotheca Historica*, ed. L. Dindorf (1868), p. 179, and in vol. 12, *Diodorus Siculus*, ed. F. R. Walton (LCL, 1967), p. 279.

other regions. They were under the leadership of worthy men of whom Danaus and Cadmus were held to be the most outstanding. The largest group, however, went out into what is now called Judaea, which is located not far from Egypt and in those days was entirely desolate. (3) A man called Moses, highly distinguished in both practical wisdom (*phronēsis*) and courage, led the migration. He took possession of the region and founded a number of cities, among them the one named Jerusalem which is now the most famous. He also dedicated the temple most honored by them, introduced the ritual and worship of the deity, and legislated and regulated the political affairs. He divided the people into twelve tribes because it corresponded to the number of months in the year. (4) He did not fabricate any image of the gods because he believed that god was not anthropomorphic; rather the heaven which encompassed the earth was the only god and lord of all. He established sacrifices and a way of living different from those of other nations; on account of his own banishment, he introduced a way of life which was somewhat unsocial and hostile to foreigners. He selected those who were the most accomplished and capable of governing the entire people and appointed them as priests; he assigned them to be responsible for the temple as well as the sacrifices to and worship of the deity. (5) He appointed the same men as judges of the most important cases and handed over to them the preservation of the laws and customs. There was never to be a king of the Jews, but the rule of the people was forever to be passed on to that priest who was held to be the most outstanding in practical wisdom and excellence. They call this man the chief priest and consider him to be the messenger to them of the divine commandments. (6) He says that this priest issues the orders (of the deity), in the assemblies and other gatherings and that in this respect the Jews are so obedient that they fall on the ground and worship the priest who has interpreted (the divine commandments) for them. At the end of the laws the following is written: "Moses heard these things from God and announced them to the Jews." The lawgiver also applied considerable foresight to military matters; he required the young men to practice courage, perseverance and in general endurance in the fate of every adversity. (7) He also directed campaigns against neighboring peoples. Having acquired considerable territory, he divided it into lots, giving equal shares to the common people and larger lots to the priests so that by receiving a higher income they could be continuously uninhibited in their devotion to the worship of the deity. It was illegal for the common people to sell their lots lest some might buy up the lots through greed and thus harass the poor and bring about a decline in the population. (8) He forced the inhabitants to raise their children and because of the meager expenses involved in raising children, the nation of the Jews has always been well populated. Concerning marriage and the burial of the dead, he established practises different from those of other men. Under the subsequent domination of the Persians and of the Macedonians who deposed them and as a result of intermingling with foreigners, many of the traditional practises of the Jews were altered.

. . . Hecataeus of Miletus narrated these things about the Jews.[8]

The introduction to the story is obviously derived from an Egyptian tradition about the expulsion from Egypt of all foreigners, whose alien religious practices had offended the gods and caused them to bring about a pestilential plague in the land. Thus in its present form the story is directed at all foreigners in Egypt, not just the Jews. Unlike later versions of the same story whose explicit purpose is to denigrate Moses and the Jews, Hecataeus' account is interested primarily in claiming superiority of Egypt over the nations of Greece and Judea. While the story distinguishes between the Greeks, who are called "the most outstanding and active" of the exiles, and the Jews, who are simply the remaining crowd, this distinction is only natural in the present form of the account which is written from a Greek point of view. The basic contrast remains that of Egyptians with Greeks and Jews.

A question arises immediately concerning the relation of this passage to similar passages in Diodorus (1.28.1–29.5; cf. 1.55.5 and 1.94.1 ff.). In 1.28 Diodorus attributes to "the Egyptians" an account of the same foreign settlements which is similar to our passage in several respects, except that the expulsion motif is entirely lacking. In 1.28 the settlements are described as colonies (*apoikiai*) sent out by the Egyptians. On the basis of the similarities between 1.28 f. and our passage, W. Jaeger and F. Jacoby are undoubtedly correct in seeing Hecataeus' influence here. The similarities relate to form as well as content: Danaus is named as the leader of the Greeks; Jews and Greeks are mentioned together; the actions of the lawgivers, especially of Belus in 28.1, are similar to those ascribed to Moses in 40; the term *apoikia* occurs in both passages. The problem is to explain the

[8] Although Photius attributes the passage to Hecataeus of Miletus (*fl. ca.* 500 B.C.E.), there is virtual unanimity among critics that the real author is the later and lesser-known Hecataeus of Abdera; see the arguments in Jaeger, "Greeks and Jews," p. 139, n. 37, and Jacoby, FGH 3a:46 f. The Roman author Aelian provides an excellent example of how such a confusion could have arisen. In his *De Natura Animalium* 11.1 he mentions the later Hecataeus and adds the comment, "not the Milesian but the Abderitan." Aelian's remark indicates that he wished to avert the very confusion that occurs in Photius.

28

differences, i.e., the absence of the expulsion motif in 1.28. Jacoby sees the account in 40 as a variant of the colonization story in 1.28 f. which Diodorus has removed from its original position; 28.1 ff. is an older version which idealizes the picture of ancient Egypt and is based on a priestly tradition that Egypt was the source of Greek and Jewish civilization. The variant form of this story in 40, according to Jacoby, shows none of these idealizing tendencies and is not concerned to prove the relationship of foreign cultures to Egypt.[9] In the main Jacoby's analysis is correct, although it seems clear that the variant form in 40 is also interested in relating Egypt to other nations. Thus Hecataeus knew and recorded two versions of a story concerning the departure of foreigners from Egypt. Both versions represent well-attested Egyptian attitudes, the one hostile toward foreigners (40), and the other, to be seen as an apologetic counterpart of the former, claiming that all culture originated in Egypt (28.1).[10] Diodorus took over both accounts. He utilized the idealizing tradition in his account of ancient Egypt in Book 1. The pestilence tradition he incorporated into his excursus on the Jews, for in his own time it had become traditional to explain Jewish origins by reciting the story of their expulsion from Egypt (see below, chapter 3).

This variant form of the tradition, however, has not influenced the picture of Moses in any substantial manner. He is characterized as "highly distinguished in both practical wisdom and courage" (*phronēsei te kai andreia polu diapherōn*[11]), which places him among the

---

[9] FGH 3a: 50 f.

[10] For a full discussion of these two attitudes and their origins in Egyptian history, see Th. Hopfner, *Orient und griechische Philosophie* (1925), ch. 3, where he discusses the contrast between the two periods in the light of Hellenistic traditions about the oriental origins of Greek philosophy. He argues that in the period prior to Alexander the Great, contacts between Greece and Egypt were limited and characterized by Egyptian hostility toward the Greeks. In the early Hellenistic period, however, when enormous new territory was opened up by Alexander, Greeks and non-Greeks were thrown into close contact. One result of and reaction to these new contacts on the part of non-Greeks was the development of elaborate theories concerning the non-Greek origins of Greek culture. Although traces of similar ideas are already present in Herodotus (2.118 ff.), they flourished and spread especially in the Hellenistic period; on the whole problem, see also M. Braun, *History and Romance in Graeco-Oriental Literature* (1938).

[11] On *phronēsis* as a distinctively political virtue, see Arist., *Pol.* 1277a, 15. Philo is also familiar with the figure of the lawgiver as an all-virtuous person: "I am not unaware that whoever is to be the best lawgiver must possess all virtues in the highest degree" (*Mos.* 2.8).

29

great lawgivers of ancient Egypt, for elsewhere Diodorus uses similar terms to describe ancient Egyptian lawgivers: Mneves (1.94.1) is "great in soul and in his life the most generous of lawgivers"; Sasychis (1.94.3) is a man "distinguished in understanding"; and Bocchoris (1.94.5) is a "wise man, distinguished in craftiness." The comparison is made even more explicit in the same passage (1.94.1 ff.). where Diodorus discusses the authority of the Egyptian lawgivers. After naming Mneves, who claimed to have received his laws from the god Hermes, Diodorus introduces a list of non-Egyptian lawgivers who likewise claimed divine origin and authority for their laws: Minos called on Zeus, Lycurgus on Apollo, Zarathustres on *agathos daimon,* Zalmoxis of the Getae on Hestia,[12] and Moses on Iao. The question is whether this list derives from Hecataeus. E. Norden thinks that it does,[13] whereas K. Reinhardt prefers Poseidonius.[14] While no final answer is possible, we can at least dispose of Reinhardt's objections against Hecataeus. His assertion that Hecataeus did not compare Moses with other figures is sufficiently refuted by the presence of Danaus and Cadmus alongside Moses in Diod. Sic. 40.3.2. With respect to Iao, he says that Hecataeus never mentioned Egyptian and presumably other foreign gods by their foreign names. This is not so. Plutarch, *De Is. et Os.* 354D, specifically states that Hecataeus of Abdera mentioned the god Amoun. As for the term Iao itself, its earliest attestation by a pagan author is Varro (d. 27 B.C.E.),[15] but there is no objection to assuming that it was already in use in Hecataeus' time. In the papyrus fragments from the sixth and fifth-century B.C.E. Jewish settlement at Elephantine, the god worshiped by the community is called *YHW,* which can be transcribed as Yahu or Yaho.[16] In either case the Greek transcription would have been Iaō or something close to it.[17] Although the Elephantine community

---

[12] Zalmoxis is said to have lived as a man among the Getae and later to have been elevated to a divine status (Herod. 4.95 f.). Strabo (7.3.5) calls him Zamolxis and says that he is the god among the Getae (16.2.39 f.).

[13] E. Norden, "Jahve und Moses," p. 300.

[14] K. Reinhardt, *Poseidonios über Ursprung und Entartung der Kultur* (1928), pp. 56-60.

[15] Lydus, *Mens.* 4.53; "The Roman Varro . . . says that he [the god of the Jews] is called *Iao* by the Chaldeans in the mysteries."

[16] A. Cowley, *Aramaic Papyri of the Fifth Century* B.C. (1923), p. xviii; and E. G. Kraeling, *The Brooklyn Museum Aramaic Papyri* (1953), pp. 84 ff.

[17] See the discussion in Ganschinietz, "Iao," RE 9 (1916): 699-703; Goodenough, *Jewish Symbols,* 2:192; and H. v. Geisau, "Iao," *Kleine Pauly,* 2 (1967): 1314 f.

ceased to exist around 400 B.C.E., some of its members must have dispersed to other cities and towns in Egypt. Furthermore, we have evidence, in the form of Aramaic papyri from around 300 B.C.E., that Aramaic-speaking Jews were resident in Egypt at that time, possibly at Thebes.[18] Thus if we assume that Hecataeus were inquiring as to the native name of the Jewish god, there is good reason to suppose that he would have heard the name Iao.[19] To be sure this does not prove that Hecataeus knew and used this form of the divine name. It merely suggests that he could have known it, a fact which earlier scholars have not recognized.

Following his description of Moses as a traditional lawgiver and as founder of the colony in Jerusalem, Hecataeus presents an extensive account of Moses' legislative activity. The laws fall into two categories, religious and social, and in both instances they are made to conform to standard Greek models. The variety of divine names is typically Greek (to daimonion, to theion, hoi theoi, ho theos). The justification for Moses' prohibition of images derives from Greek philosophical traditions in both its denial of anthropomorphism and its identification of the deity with the heavens and the cosmos. The following passage from Aristotle stands close to Hecataeus: "Therefore there is only one heaven. It has been handed down by the ancients . . . that these (the heavenly bodies) are gods and that the divine encircles the whole of nature" (Metaph. 1074a, 38 ff.).

Aristotle gladly accepts this ancient definition, although he too rejects the corollary that the gods exist in human form (1074b, 3 ff.). A passage in Herodotus is also strikingly similar to Moses' rejection of images. Herodotus explains that the Persians reject images because their deity is not anthropomorphic: "They dedicate no images or temples. . . . This is, I think, because they, unlike the Greeks, do not consider the gods to be like men. . . . They call Zeus the entire circle of heaven" (1.131). In spite of parallel between Hecataeus, Aristotle, and Herodotus, we need not posit a direct relationship between them.

[18] The two papyri are numbers 81 and 82 in Cowley, Aramaic Papyri, pp. 190-201; on the history of Jews in Egypt subsequent to 400 B.C.E., see Kraeling, Brooklyn Papyri, pp. 113-19.

[19] Iao also occurs in a Greek fragment from Qumran (4Q LXX Lev^b) discussed by P. W. Skehan, "The Qumran Manuscripts and Textual Criticism," in Volume du Congrès, Strasbourg 1956 (Suppl. to Vetus Testamentum 4, 1957), pp. 149-60 (esp. p. 157). Skehan dates the papyrus to the first century B.C.E.

Their likeness can be understood as independent attempts by educated Greeks to explain the rejection of images in the sophisticated terms of Greek religious language. Beyond this, A. D. Nock says that the ascription to non-Greeks of a reaction to anthropomorphism "became something of an ethnographic commonplace." [20]

The first section of the excursus closes with a reference to the written Mosaic laws: "And at the conclusion of the laws it is written, Moses heard these words from God and spoke them to the Jews." Various texts have been put forward as the basis for this reference. Jaeger suggests Deut. 28:69 (29:1 LXX) ;[21] Reinach mentions Lev. 26:46 and 27:34.[22] In addition one should also consider Deut. 32:44 (LXX), which comes at the end of the Pentateuch and might thus explain "at the conclusion of the laws" in Hecataeus' text. Actually, all these passages are versions of a common summary formula, and each bears an almost equal resemblance to Hecataeus' reference. At the time of his writing, however, there was probably no complete written translation of the Pentateuch, although the Jewish community in Alexandria must have used informal Greek translations (targums) in their synagogue worship.[23] Thus Hecataeus' "quotation" is probably a paraphrase of the summary formula as transmitted to him orally by Jewish acquaintances in Alexandria.

The social-political aspect of Moses' legislative activity begins with the founding of the cities, including Jerusalem, and the division of the people into twelve tribes. Although neither of these activities is attributed to Moses in the Jewish scriptures, where he is forbidden to cross the Jordan, Philo does make him responsible for the twelve tribes. Philo's justification of the number twelve is similar to that of Hecataeus: "Twelve is the perfect number . . . the path of the sun attests to this. For it completes its circuit in twelve months" (*De fug.* 184 ff.) . Even more interesting is a statement in Plato's *Laws:* "And the legislator must apportion the men into twelve parts and arrange the rest of the goods into twelve parts which shall be as equal as possible"

[20] Nock, "Posidonius," JRS 49 (1959) : 6.
[21] "Greeks and Jews," p. 139. The text as printed reads "Deuteronomy 29:7."
[22] Reinach, *Textes,* p. 18, n. 2.
[23] The translation of the Pentateuch is normally set sometime in the third century B.C.E. Cf. P. Kahle, *The Cairo Geniza* (1959²), pp. 209-14; F. M. Cross, "The History of the Biblical Text in the Light of the Discoveries in the Judean Desert," HTR 57 (1964) : 281-99; and P. W. Skehan, "The Biblical Scrolls from Qumran and the Text of the Old Testament," BA 28 (1965) : 87-100, esp. pp. 94 ff.

(745D). Plato's dictum agrees with Hecataeus not only in settling on twelve as the most suitable number, but also in recognizing the ideal of distributing equal shares of property to all citizens. Here again Moses' legislation is brought into harmony with the tradition of philosophical Greek lawgivers.

The bulk of Moses' social legislation is described in 40.3.6-8. In 6 f. he is pictured as a wise military leader. As such he instituted a rigorous training program for the youth, which is vaguely reminiscent of the training received by the guardians in Plato's *Republic* (375 ff., 390). 40.3.7 covers Moses' successful campaigns in the surrounding territory, as the result of which he distributed equal lots to the common people and larger lots to the priests. In Hecataeus' account Moses alone has assumed the task of the conquest and distribution of the land, a task which he shares with Joshua in the Jewish scriptures (Josh. 12:1-24). Concerning priestly lots, the biblical narrative is of at least two opinions. Josh. 13:14, 32 f., and 14:3 explicitly exclude the priests as recipients of any land except their residential cities. Conversely, Ezek. 48:8-13 is quite explicit concerning the location and dimensions of the priestly allotments, and 48:14 even prohibits priests from selling or exchanging their allotments.

Hecataeus' version clearly stands closer to Ezekiel, but need not derive from it. Both undoubtedly reflect the political situation of postexilic Palestine when the priests ruled the people and the temple in Jerusalem had accumulated considerable wealth and lands. This political situation probably lies behind the statement that Moses provided the priests with larger lots as well as the earlier statement that Moses appointed priests to rule the people.

Hecataeus' justification of the unequal distribution of lots and the prohibitions against selling them follows his regular practice of offering rational explanations for anything slightly out of the ordinary.[24] These explanations serve to reinforce his picture of the ideal Mosaic state: the leaders are relieved of all mundane concerns, and the citizens are protected by law from "capitalistic entrepreneurs." The former finds its counterpart in Plato, *Rep.* 540A-B, where the primary

[24] This rationalism was not limited to Hecataeus, but was rather a common trait of Hellenistic ethnography. Cf. A. Dihle, "Zur hellenistischen Ethnographie," in *Grecs et Barbares* (1961), pp. 207 ff. This rationalism often took the form of reducing all cultural pecularities to differences in climate, e.g., Aristotle, *Pol.* 1327b, 23 ff., and Polybius, 4.21.

duty of the legislator-philosopher is the study of philosophy, while protection of citizens against poverty and the prohibition against depriving a citizen of his allotted property are discussed in the *Laws* 744. Like Plato, Hecataeus' Moses accepts as the ideal that every man should have equal possessions, although in practice he is willing to make certain concessions. Like Plato, he refused to allow the sale of the citizen's basic allotment.

In section 7 Moses' prohibition against selling lots is presented as a means not only of protecting the poor but also of maintaining the population level. This theme is pursued in the following line, where it is said that he required the inhabitants to raise their children. The result of this particular requirement, says Hecataeus, is that the Jews have always been a populous nation. Here again Hecataeus' account diverges from the Jewish scriptures but finds a parallel in later Jewish sources. Although there is no prohibition against infanticide or child exposure in the Jewish scriptures, Josephus writes that the law of Moses "commands that all children be brought up." [25] Why, one may ask, did Hecataeus see fit to mention this seemingly trivial matter? The answer, I think, is that the question of population control had become an important concern of Greek political philosophy.[26] Thus the fact that Moses had implicitly forbidden child exposure provided yet another example of his status as a philosophical legislator.

Hecataeus' final comment concerns marriage and burial customs. In its present form the narrative simply states that Moses' regulations were substantially different from those of other men. It is probably safe to assume that Diodorus has condensed Hecataeus at this point, although it is impossible to determine how extensive the original discussion may have been.[27]

[25] *Ap.* 2.202. The reference is probably to the command in Genesis, "Be fruitful and multiply" (Gen. 1:22 etc.). The issue of Jewish population in relation to the care for raising all children seems to have interested pagan authors. Strabo mentions that the Egyptians and the Jews raise all their children (17.2.5), and Tacitus calls attention to the same practice among the Jews (*Hist.* 5.5).

[26] Aristotle discusses the problem frequently. In *Pol.* 1335b, 19 ff., the question of population control is discussed just as in our passage, in connection with the practice of child exposure.

[27] If, as seems possible, we are dealing with an abbreviation of the original, either Diodorus or Photius may have been responsible. Recent studies by J. Palm, *Über Sprache u. Stil des Diodorus von Sizilien* (1955); R. Laqueur, "Diodorea," *Hermes* 86 (1958): 257-90; and M. Spoerri, *Späthellenistische Berichte über Welt, Kultur und Götter: Untersuchungen zu Diodor von Sizilien* (1959) have shown

This concluding remark brings us to Hecataeus' general assessment of Moses. In section 4 he characterizes the Jewish cult and civilization as "different" (*exēllagmenos*), and their culture as "somewhat unsocial and hostile to foreigners" (*apanthrōpos tis kai misoxenos*). These terms represent the only negative comments in the entire narrative, and even they are somewhat modified. The indefinite *tis* with *apanthrōpos* should probably be translated to read "somewhat unsocial," and the Jewish position as a whole is justified by Hecataeus as a defensive reaction by the Jews to their own banishment from Egypt. In addition, the terms *exēllagmenos* and *parēllagmenos*, which Jacoby interprets as terms of deprecation, mean nothing more than "different" and "unusual," without any overtones of negative judgment. In 1.94.1 Diodorus uses *exēllagmenos* and *paradoxos* to describe Egyptian customs; in 1.27.1 he refers especially to their marriage practices as *para to koinon ethos*. In neither case is there a negative judgment. Such expressions were characteristic of ethnographic excurses from the early Ionians onward, and it was the regular practice of ethnographic writers to include a section on *thaumasia* and *nomima barbarika*.[28] Jacoby fails to take sufficient account of this particular literary genre and thus concludes that Hecataeus regarded Judaism as a strange phenomenon.[29] Jaeger, I think, is closer to the mark:

Hecataeus' aspect of Jewish life (*bios*) is quite congruent with his approach to Egyptian history. As a court historian of the first Hellenistic king of Egypt he is concerned with the problem of authoritative government. . . . Besides the ancient Egyptian monarchy, the Jewish system offered to Hecataeus another example of such an authoritarian government, and this new example was all the more interesting because it seemed to have a striking resemblance to Plato's ideal state. . . . Hecataeus immediately discovers in

---

that Diodorus regularly reworked his sources in both style and content. Lacking evidence to the contrary, we should probably assume that the judgment applies here as well. Photius shows considerable variety in his treatment of sources. Some are noted briefly, while others are quoted at length. The use of the first person in the opening sentence ("Since we are about to narrate . . .") indicates that Photius was probably quoting from Diodorus. On Photius' method of treating his sources, see Dvornik, *Patriarch Photius*, pp. 6 f., and the new critical edition of Photius, now in progress, *Photius Bibliothèque*, ed. R. Henry, I (1959) : xx ff.

[28] Cf. K. Trüdinger, *Studien zur Geschichte der griechisch-römischen Ethnographie* (1918), pp. 44 ff., 106 ff. Aristotle is known to have written a work entitled *Nomima Barbarika*.

[29] FGH 3a: 48 ("nur als fremdartig").

Moses' legislation such an ideal scheme of human education. The whole system is based on bravery, endurance (*karteria*) and self-discipline. . . . One virtue is lacking: wisdom, which is identical with piety. This virtue is represented in the Jewish scheme by the highest class of the Mosaic state, the priests—for the whole scheme is aristocratic through and through. . . . It is the picture of a "philosophical race" in the sense of the contemporary main currents of Greek intellectual life.[30]

Jaeger's assessment of the excursus as a kind of political utopia sheds additional light on the formal structure of the passage which marks it as a typical example of Hellenistic ethnography. We have already noted the interest in rational explanation, a characteristic of Hellenistic and particularly Peripatetic ethnography. This led inevitably to frequent idealizations of peoples and practices, a trait which appears in Hecataeus' account of Moses.[31] Concerning the types of information which were included in such ethnographies and the manner in which they were ordered, K. Trüdinger has made the following observations: the pre-Herodotian Ionian ethnographers had developed a fixed form, with fixed *topoi*, which is still visible in Herodotus' ethnographic excurses.[32] Three themes occur in practically every case: religious laws, including the conception of the deity and the types of sacrifices; next, unusual customs including special marriage customs; and finally, burial practices.[33] It can hardly be a coincidence

[30] Jaeger, "Greeks and Jews," pp. 141 ff. In *Diokles,* pp. 134 ff., Jaeger has shown that this picture of the Jews as a race of philosophers persisted within the Peripatetic school for a number of years. Theophrastus (*apud* Porphyry, *Abst.* 2.26) refers to the Jews as "a people of philosophers" because they continually discuss the deity and contemplate the heavens at night. In addition, the diplomat Megasthenes (*apud* Clem. Alex., *Strom.* 1. [15.] 72.5) says the following on non-Greek philosophers: "Everything which the ancients have spoken about nature has also been said by philosophers outside of Greece, in India by the Brahmans and in Syria by those who are called Jews." Clearchus of Soli (*apud* Josephus, *Ap.* 1.176 ff.) relates that Aristotle had met and conversed with a thoroughly hellenized Jew in Coele-Syria. According to Clearchus, Aristotle described the Jews as "descendants of the philosophers in India; among the Indians philosophers are said to be called Kalanoi, among the Syrians Jews." Finally, Hermippus (*apud* Josephus, *Ap.* 1.165) concludes his presentation of Pythagoras' system with these words: "He did and said these things in imitation of the ideas of the Jews and the Thracians."

[31] For a discussion of this trait in ethnographic writings see Dihle, "Ethnographie," pp. 209 and 226 ff.

[32] E.g., 2.2 ff. on Egypt, 3.20 ff. on Ethiopia, 3.98 ff. on India, and 4.17 ff. on the North countries.

[33] Trüdinger, *Studien,* pp. 21 ff.

that these three themes occur in precisely this order in Hecataeus' account of Moses.

In the early Hellenistic period and especially under the influence of Aristotle and the Peripatetics, Trüdinger notes the emergence of three additional elements in Greek ethnography: the concern for political institutions, as typified by Plato's *Republic* and Aristotle's *Politics;* a new concern for the historical origins of various peoples; and an interest in the distinctiveness of foreign peoples.[34] The last element in particular is evident in the contrast between Hecataeus and Herodotus. Whereas the latter was generally content to describe the customs of foreign peoples, Hecataeus attempted to relate them to individual lawgivers.[35]

Together with the traditional elements inherited from the Ionian tradition, these special Hellenistic features account for the full structure of Hecataeus' excursus and confirm our view of it as a typical example of early Hellenistic ethnography of the type noted by Jaeger and Jacoby.[36]

A word remains to be said about Hecataeus' sources. The contribution of Greek ethnography and its idealizing tendencies to the form and content of the passage has been established. It has also been shown that the historical introduction (40.3.1-2) derives ultimately from Egyptian sources.[37] In addition it must be assumed that Hecataeus knew and conversed with Greek-speaking Jews in Alexandria.[38] From these contacts he derived his information about Jewish history and culture as well as his paraphrase of the material from the Pentateuch. No doubt this information was already reworked and idealized for apologetic purposes (see below, pp. 76 ff.), but the final form of the excursus is due to Hecataeus who shaped the material in accordance with his own philsophical, political, and literary ends.

[34] *Studien,* pp. 44 f. and 74 ff., where he notes the same elements in Megasthenes.
[35] In this he was undoubtedly influenced by Aristotle, for in *Pol.* 1274a, 23 ff. Aristotle gives an extensive list of lawgivers with a brief description of their characteristic laws; cf. Diod. Sic. 1.28.1 and 1.94.1 ff.
[36] "Sie beschreibt ein Volk nicht um seiner selbst willen, sondern verwendet das historisch-ethnographische Material als Substrat, um ein Staatsideal oder eine andere philosophische Theorie an einem fiktiven oder wirklichen Volke durchzuführen . . ." (FGH 3a:29).
[37] Jacoby, FGH 3a:50.
[38] So Jaeger, "Greeks and Jews," p. 139; *Diokles,* p. 143 n. 1, and p. 146; Jacoby, FGH 3a:51; and Nock, "Posidonius," p. 9.

Poseidonius of Apamea—Strabo of Amaseia

The next extensive discussion of Moses as a philosophical lawgiver appears almost 300 years after Hecataeus in book 16 of Strabo's *Geography*.[39] This text has been widely, if not quite unanimously, attributed to Poseidonius, and for this reason I have included it under the heading Poseidonius-Strabo:[40]

Although they [the inhabitants of Judaea] are thus of mixed origins, the predominant report of those currently held concerning the temple in Jerusalem affirms that the Egyptians are the ancestors of those people who are now called Jews.

(35) For a certain Moses, who was one of the Egyptian priests, held a section of what is called the <lower>[41] region (*chōra*). But he became dissatisfied with the way of life and departed thence to Jerusalem, in the company of many who worshipped the deity. For he said and taught that the Egyptians, as well as the Libyans, were deluded in likening the deity to wild animals and cattle. Nor did the Greeks do well in fashioning gods in human form. For that which encompasses us all, including earth and sea—that which we call the heavens, the world and the essence of things—this one thing only is god. And what man in his right mind would dare to fabricate an image of this god in the likeness of some mortal being? Rather we should forsake all such image-making and instead set apart a sacred precinct and a worthy

[39] 16.2.35-39. Before Poseidonius (d. *ca.* 50 B.C.E), Polybius is known to have discussed the Jews and the temple in Jerusalem in connection with his account of Antiochus III's successful campaigns in Syria and Palestine. Josephus (*AJ* 12.136) quotes from Book 16 of Polybius' *Histories*: ". . . after a short time the Jews who live near the temple which is called Ierosolyma also came over to him; of this temple we have more to say, especially concerning the renown of the temple, but we will put off this account till a later time." Concerning the content of the excursus we possess no information whatsoever beyond Josephus' excerpt.

[40] Among those who attribute the passage to Poseidonius are: Reinach, *Textes*, p. 99, n. 2; Norden, "Jahve und Moses," pp. 296 ff.; K. Reinhardt, *Poseidonios über Ursprung*, pp. 6 ff.; I. Heinemann, "Poseidonios über die Entwicklung der jüdischen Religion," MGWJ 62 (1919) : 111 ff.; *idem*, "Antisemitismus," RE Suppl. 5 (1931) : 34 f.; Jacoby, FGH 2C: 196 ff. Nock, "Posidonius," pp. 6 ff., seems to waver between Poseidonius and Strabo. Schürer 1:156, sees a Jewish source with Stoic influence. W. Aly, *Strabonis Geographica* 4: *Strabon von Amaseia* (1957) : 191 ff., disputes the traditional attribution altogether. M. Laffranque, *Poseidonios d'Apamée* (1964) does not mention the passage at all.

[41] The word *katō* ("lower") was first added by A. Coray in his edition of 1815 and has been generally accepted by subsequent editors. *Chōra* is a technical term used to designate the territory outside Alexandria. In addition, *anō* and *katō* were sometimes used to distinguish Upper and Lower Egypt; cf. Liddell-Scott, *s.v. chōra* II.3. Whether Strabo intended to be so specific is uncertain.

sanctuary for worship without images. Some people with auspicious dreams should sleep in the temple for their own benefit and others should sleep there for the benefit of others. Those who live wisely and justly should always expect some good thing or sign or gift from god, although others should not.

(36) In so speaking, Moses persuaded not a few reasonable men and led them to the place where the settlement of Jerusalem is now located. He took it easily since the region was not desirable or such that anyone would be eager to fight for it. The area was rocky, and although the city itself was well-watered, the surrounding country was dry, arid and, within a radius of sixty stadia, rocky as well. At the same time he put forward (as a defense) the cult and the deity instead of arms, thinking it (more) worth while to seek a sanctuary for the deity and promising to set up a ritual and a cult which would not burden the adherents with expenses, divine ecstasies or other foolish practices. Thus Moses set up an excellent government (archē), as a result of which the surrounding peoples were won over on account of their association with him and the advantages which were offered.

(37) . . . . (38) . . . .

(39) . . . Such were also Moses and his successors, who set out from good beginnings but took a serious turn for the worse.

Book 16 of Strabo's *Geography* contains his description of the countries between India and the Mediterranean. In 16.2.34 he begins his account of Judaea, noting especially that the inhabitants of the region represent a population comprised of Egyptian, Arabian, and Phoenician tribes. Concerning the ethnographic origins of the Jews in particular, Strabo reports that a number of explanations were in existence at his time. Like Tacitus,[42] he observes that the most prevalent of these theories was that the Jews were descendants of the Egyptians. Apart from Pompeius Trogus (see below, pp. 48 ff.) and the anonymous opinions cited by Tacitus, pagan authors agreed unanimously in this respect.

As proof of the Egyptian origin of the Jews, Strabo introduces his account of Moses and the founding of the Jewish religion. It was not Strabo's wont to relate the early history of the peoples whom he described.[43] Thus whatever else we may say about the content of the excursus, we should not forget that its stated purpose is to substantiate the common pagan belief, shared by Strabo, in the Egyptian origins of the Jews.

[42] Tacitus, *Hist.* 5.2, lists five different theories concerning Jewish origins.
[43] 10.4.8-9 on Crete is the one notable exception.

Moses is described as one of the priests from lower Egypt. In comparison with Hecataeus this description represents a *novum*. Its ultimate roots are to be found in the tradition, reflected already by Hecataeus, that the Jews were expelled from Egypt as the result of a plague. More immediately, it is a version of the anti-Jewish accounts of figures like Lysimachus and Apion which made the Jews descendants of exiled Egyptian lepers. In Strabo's account not only are the Jews as a people of Egyptian origin, but their leader was an Egyptian priest. Strabo probably encountered this tradition during his prolonged sojourn in Egypt (2.3.5). In the course of his trips and conversations in Heliopolis, as well as Alexandria, he must have heard and read of Moses as part of the local propaganda.[44]

The existence of such traditions about Moses as an Egyptian priest is attested by Manetho and Apion (see below, pp. 113 ff.). In Josephus, *Ap.* 1.250 f., Pseudo-Manetho identifies Osarsiph, an ancient priest of Heliopolis, with Moses. Josephus (*Ap.* 2.10) attributes a similar statement to Apion: "Moses, as I have heard from the elders (*presbuteroi*) of the Egyptians, was an Heliopolitan. . . ." Two facts emerge from these remarks of Manetho and Apion: first, that Moses was known among certain Egyptians as a local priest of Heliopolis and second, that the tradition existed already in the first century B.C.E., that is, before the time of Strabo. Strabo also adds the remark that Moses "held a section of what is called the *chōra*" (see above, n. 41). While this seems to imply a jurisdictional responsibility of some sort, it is impossible to determine whether the writer meant to specify political or cultic authority. In either case, it is assumed that he held a position of some authority.

Nonetheless, says Strabo, Moses became disenchanted with conditions in Egypt and departed for Judaea. There is no mention of the expulsion story as in practically every other pagan author. In particular, Moses' motive was dissatisfaction with the Egyptian understanding of the deity, i.e., theological in the proper sense. He faults the Egyptians and the Libyans for likening the deity to animals[45]

---

[44] Cf. 17.1.29 where Strabo describes his trip to Heliopolis. It was on such a trip to Heliopolis that a certain Chaeremon undertook to "explain" the great fame of that ancient city. On the significant presence of Jews at Heliopolis, notably the Jewish general Onias and his troops, see the discussion in CPJ 1:20 f.

[45] On a later Jewish reaction to Egyptian animal worship, see Wisdom of Solomon 11:15 ff.

and the Greeks for fashioning images of the deity in human form. In contrast he proposes his own definition: "God is the one thing which encompasses us all, including heaven and earth," to which Strabo adds: "which we call heaven and earth and the essence (*physis*) of things." In effect there are two definitions, one attributed to Moses and one which is Strabo's own paraphrase of the former. The latter is clearly Stoic[46] while the former is reminiscent of Moses' view of god according to Hecataeus (see above, pp. 31 ff.).[47] It is the same basic, though somewhat expanded, formula which is at least as old as Aristotle and which enjoyed a wide circulation in Strabo's time.[48]

A second point of contact between Strabo and Hecataeus is the Mosaic rejection of images. In Hecataeus the reason was that the deity is not anthropomorphic. In Strabo, Moses criticizes the Egyptians because they represent the deity as theriomorphic and the Greeks because they make anthropomorphic images of the gods. As in the case of Hecataeus, whose account may well have influenced Strabo,[49] Moses here serves as the spokesman for traditional criticism of anthropomorphic religion, both Greek and Egyptian.[50]

The final segment of the theological section deals with dream oracles in the temple. According to Jacoby, who claims that the lines do not fit the present context, Strabo himself inserted the passage into his source.[51] On the other side, Norden, Reinhardt, and Aly agree that it properly belongs here.[52] As Reinhardt notes, the question of oracles is one of the points of comparison between Moses and other

---

[46] "Zeno says that the substance of god is the whole world and the heaven . . . so also (say) Chrysippus . . . and Poseidonius" (Diog. Laert. 7.148; cf. 7.138). Reinhardt (*Ursprung*, p. 9), who regards Poseidonius as Strabo's source, paraphrases the passage as follows: ". . . das Uns-Umfangende, das In- und Ausser-Mir, der Makrokosmos, der den Mikrokosmos in sich trägt und hält." Surely this is an over-interpretation which does a serious injustice to Strabo's words. When we consider Strabo's paraphrase separately, we need see in it nothing more than a common Stoic formula.

[47] So Reinhardt, *Ursprung*, pp. 9 f.; Nock, "Posidonius," p. 8; and Aly, *Strabon*, pp. 197 f.

[48] Cf. Reinhardt, *Ursprung*, pp. 10 f. for other examples of this expanded form.

[49] So Jacoby, FGH 2C:198.

[50] On anthropomorphism, see the debate between Origen and Celsus (*c. Cels.* 1.5) where Origen quotes a series of Greek authors to support his rejection of anthropomorphism. The attack on Egyptian animal worship was shared equally by Greeks (Sext. Emp., *Pyr.* 3.219) and Jews (Josephus, *Ap.* 2.81).

[51] FGH 2C:198.

[52] Norden, "Jahve und Moses," p. 293, n. 1; Reinhardt, *Ursprung*, p. 14; Aly, *Strabon*, pp. 192 f.

figures in 39. As Strabo himself says, the two types of dream oracles are typically Greek, though the general practice was found throughout the ancient world.[53] Thus in the concluding statement of the section, Moses is once again the spokesman for a typically Stoic dogma, the belief that the gods benefit those who live righteously but not those who live otherwise. Such righteous and moderate persons should always expect good things from the gods.

The third section describes Moses' followers and the territory where they settled.[54] Strabo portrays Moses not only as a superior theologian but also as a successful and influential teacher. As such he persuaded his people to leave Egypt and its inferior religion. Thus instead of deploying military defenses,[55] Moses turned his attention to dedicating a sanctuary and establishing a cult which would not burden its adherents with expensive contributions or other foolish activities. Here again Strabo reflects the language of long-established theological and philosophical traditions. The idea that the gods were not honored by extravagant offerings is associated especially, though not exclusively, with the Pythagoreans. Diodorus Siculus quotes the Pythagorean lawgiver Saleucus as counseling purity of soul "because the gods do not take pleasure in the sacrifices and extravagant expenses of evil men but in the just and good practices of upright men" (12. 20.2). Iamblichus attributes a similar statement to Porphyry: "The Olympians attend to the disposition of those who sacrifice, not to the amount of things sacrificed" (*Vit. Pyth.* 27.122). In short, Strabo's Moses shares with these lawgivers the rejection of cultic extravagance.

In the concluding lines of this section Strabo mentions Moses' suc-

[53] 17.1.17: "It contains the temple of Serapis which is honored with much reverence and brings about cures, with the result that even the most reliable men believe in it and sleep there—*some for themselves and some for others.*"

[54] The description of Jerusalem is similar in some respects to the report of Timochares in Eusebius, *Praep. Evang.* 9.35.1 (452a-c). On the other hand there must have been many brief descriptions of Jerusalem, and it is noteworthy that Strabo and Timochares agree on those points (rocky surrounding, difficulty of access, plenty of water) which are geographically accurate. The figures for the circumference of the city vary considerably: Strabo has 60 stadia, Timochares and Aristeas (105) have 40, "Hecataeus" (*apud* Josephus, *Ap.* 1.197) 50, Josephus (*BJ* 5.159) 33, and the "surveyor of Syria" (Eusebius, *Praep. Evang.* 9.36.1) 27.

[55] The metaphorical use of "weapons" was a commonplace in Greek literature. Paul (2 Cor. 6:7) uses the phrase "weapons of righteousness." A sentence from Epictetus (3.22.94) bears a close resemblance to Strabo: "to the Cynic, conscience *rather than arms* and bodyguards grants this power."

cessful political activity. Just as the beginning of 36 speaks of the "numerous reasonable men" who followed him out of Egypt, so the conclusion refers to his "excellent government" and the ease with which he won over the surrounding peoples. But in contrast to Hecataeus who pictures Moses' military conquest of the territory, Strabo's Moses relies entirely on the merits of his institutions and his diplomatic prowess.

With the completion of 36, Moses disappears for three chapters. 37 describes the decline of Judaism, as superstitious and tyrannical people assumed leadership of the people. 38 lists a number of lawgivers who claimed divine inspiration for their laws, while 39 lists a number of prophets who were deemed worthy to be kings because they transmitted commandments from the gods. At the very end of 39 Moses reappears where he is once again set apart from his later successors: "Such were also Moses and his successors, who set out from good beginnings but took a serious turn for the worse." Concerning the relationship of these two chapters to Moses, one important element must be emphasized. The lists of 38 and 39 are quite distinct. 38 concerns lawgivers proper and mentions only Minos and Lycurgus by name; 39 concerns prophets (manteis), and it is among these prophets, not the lawgivers, that Strabo places Moses. Thus although both Hecataeus and Strabo include Moses in groups of inspired figures, Strabo's list focuses on religious leaders. Indeed, Strabo makes no mention whatsoever of Moses' political legislation, whereas Hecataeus divides his attention equally between religious and the political laws.

Of the many pagan discussions of Moses, Strabo's is certainly one of the most sympathetic. Entirely lacking are references to the exodus as an expulsion, to the Jews as lepers, and to Moses as an enemy of mankind. Rather, he is pictured as an archetype of the religious and prophetic lawgiver. Significantly, traditional criticisms of the Jews as a people are reserved for Moses' successors, from whom he is sharply distinguished.[56] To explain this image of Moses we must look in two directions—Strabo's sources and the idealizing tendencies of utopian ethnographies. As did Hecataeus before him, Strabo also shows the same penchant for remaking Moses in the image of his own Stoic philosophy.

[56] Among Moses' successors, Alexander Jannaeus, Hyrcanus, and Aristobulus are mentioned by name.

Strabo or Poseidonius?

As noted above, scholars have been *almost* unanimous in identify-ing Poseidonius as Strabo's source for the Moses excursus. This attribu-tion was first made in the heyday of Quellenkritik and at a time when Poseidonius in particular was regarded as the principal source for numerous Greek and Roman authors.[57] More recently, however, the basic assumptions of this pan-Poseidonionism have been called into serious question.[58] In view of these developments in Poseidonius studies, it seems wise to reexamine briefly the attribution to Posei-donius of Strabo's excursus on Moses. The chief spokesman for this position is K. Reinhardt in his work on Poseidonius' view of history.[59] His argument centers on the following points: (1) the Mosaic defini-tion of the deity, (2) Moses' role as diviner, (3) Moses as an example of idealized ancient lawgivers, and (4) the view of history as moving from noble origins to subsequent decay.

(1) We have already seen that the terms used by Strabo to describe the Mosaic deity are characteristic of Stoicism in general (see above, pp. 41 f.). In support of his position, Reinhardt quotes a passage from Sextus Empiricus in which Poseidonius is not even mentioned: "Heraclitus said that that which encompasses us is a rational and conscious being." [60] In addition to the uncertain attribution, there is nothing in the text which would indicate a close connection to Strabo's definition.

(2) Even less convincing is the discussion of divination. He argues that Poseidonius, in contrast to earlier Stoics, had developed an elabo-rate theory of divination. But divination was a fixed dogma in the Stoic tradition, and Strabo's account presupposes nothing more than

[57] The primary figure in Poseidonius research of this period was K. Reinhardt. His works included *Poseidonios* (1921), *Kosmos und Sympathie* (1926), *Poseidonios über Ursprung und Entartung der Kultur* (1928), and an extensive article on Poseidonius in RE 41 (1953).

[58] Actually the reaction dates back as early as 1912 to an article of J. F. Robson, "The Posidonius Myth," CQ 12 (1918): 179-95. Recently, the challenge has been renewed by M. Laffranque, *Poseidonius d'Apamée* (1964), p. 44, who suggests a complete review of earlier attributions to Poseidonius; see also A. Dihle, "Ethnographie," p. 226.

[59] *Poseidonius über Ursprung.*

[60] Sextus Empiricus, *Math.* 7.127. In his earlier work, *Kosmos u. Sympathie*, pp. 196 ff., Reinhardt had undertaken to prove that Poseidonius' thought lies behind the statement which Sextus attributes to Heraclitus.

the common practice of incubation or dream oracles received by sleeping in temples. As for his statement that the wise should expect benefits from the gods, this too was a Stoic commonplace, shared by Poseidonius but in no way a distinctive characteristic of his.

(3) Both Reinhardt and Norden have assigned particular significance to the lists of lawgivers and prophets in 38-39. Both assert that Strabo's list coincides substantially with a similar list in Cicero, *Div.* 1.88 f., whose source Norden accepts as Poseidonius.[61]

CICERO	STRABO
Colchas	
Amphilochus	
Mopsus	
Amphiaraus	Amphiaraus
Teiresias	Teiresias
Priam	Trophonius
Cassandra	Orpheus
Polyidus	Musaeus
Druids	Zamolxis
	Decaeneus
	Achaecarus
	Gymnosophists
Magi	Magi and necromancers
Chaldaeans	Chaldaeans
Etrurians	Tyrrhenians[62]
	Moses

A brief examination shows that the two lists share only five items in common. The two barbarian groups in both lists, the Magi and the Chaldaeans, were also the most widely known and might be expected in any such list. In the light of these substantial differences, we are rather forced to accept Aly's conclusion that it is simply not possible to regard either list as the source of the other or both as derived from a single common list.[63]

[61] Norden, "Jahve und Moses," pp. 295 f.

[62] *Tyrrhenos* is a Greek term for Etrurian or Etruscan.

[63] Aly, *Strabon*, pp. 206 f. Reinhardt, *Ursprung*, pp. 23 ff. explains the absence of Moses' name from Cicero's list as due to the fact that Cicero used Poseidonius' earlier work *On Divination*, which did not yet include Moses, whereas Strabo used the later *Histories*. This argument becomes unnecessary once we recognize that

Two further points weaken Reinhardt's position. Seneca (*Ep.* 90.5-6) contains a list of lawgivers which is quoted explicitly from Poseidonius. In it he names Solon, Lycurgus, Zaleucus, and Charondas as praiseworthy lawgivers. In comparison, Strabo's list includes only Lycurgus. Thus where we are able to compare a text in which Poseidonius is cited by name the differences far outweigh any similarities. The second point is that traditions about prophet-kings circulated widely in Greek and Latin literature.[64] Thus there is no compelling evidence in favor of Poseidonius as the source of the list. The best solution is to assume that Strabo composed the list himself, using earlier lists as his models.

(4) Reinhardt's final argument concerns the pattern of ideal beginnings and subsequent degeneration. Here, and here alone, we are in the fortunate position of knowing that Poseidonius held such a theory. In discussing the role of philosophy in human progress, Seneca quotes Poseidonius: "In that age, which is called golden, Poseidonius holds that the government was in the control of the wise." [65] At a later time, he continues, vices arose, kingdoms were transformed into tyrannies, and a need for laws arose.

The basic objection to this argument is that the idea of the golden age, with its corollaries of ideal founders and subsequent degeneration, is in no way limited to or especially characteristic of Poseidonius. A prime example is Plato. In the *Rep.* 544C he lists four common types of government, of which tyranny is the last and worst. In the following paragraphs he then details the characteristics of each and the gradual decline from the highest form, aristocracy, to the lowest, tyranny.[66] The idea persisted in later writers, among them Polybius who includes in his history the theory of six types of governments and the path of their systematic degeneration (6.4.5–6.9.14). Finally, the pattern occurs elsewhere in Strabo's *Geography*. Quite similar to our passage is 10.4.8-9, where Strabo contrasts the good laws of ancient Crete with its subsequent turn for the worse and the rise of piracy.

---

the list was probably composed by Strabo for use in its present context, and that his models made no mention of Moses at all.

[64] Herod., 4.94 f.; Plato, *Leg.* 632D; Polybius, 10.2.1 ff. etc.

[65] *Ep.* 90.5. The idea of the golden age is also present in a passage in which Athenaeus quotes Poseidonius concerning ancient Rome: "there was a wonderful devotion to the deity" (*Deipn.* 274A).

[66] Cf. Plato, *Crit.* 121AC, where a similar pattern of decay is expounded in connection with the myth of Atlantis.

Thus it must be admitted that the underlying conception of ideal beginnings and later decay is shared by many ancient authors including Poseidonius and Strabo. In the absence of any specific reference by Strabo to his source, we must be content with the conclusion that the idea could have been derived from a great variety of sources, including Strabo himself.

What then can be said about Strabo's source of information? Some have suggested a Jewish source, written or oral, which portrayed Moses in Stoic terms,[67] while others have rejected the suggestion on the grounds that no Jew could have spoken in such terms about Moses.[68] A. D. Nock suggests that the excursus "reproduces the creation of a Jew familiar with the ideas of Poseidonius, a Jew whose hellenization was not, like Philo's, controlled by an overpowering loyalty to scripture." [69]

Examples of such Jews are not difficult to find. The Jews whom Philo chides for following the allegorical to the exclusion of the literal meaning of the scriptures (*Mig.* 89 f.), the hellenizing Jews of 1 Macc. 1:11 ff. and 2 Macc. 4:7-20, who built a gymnasium in Jerusalem, undid their circumcision, and renamed the city Antioch;[70] the Jewish apologist Artapanus, who does not hesitate to credit Moses with the foundation of the animal-worshiping Egyptian religion[71]—all are typical of the Judaism described by Nock. Such Jews must have existed in every Greek city and especially in Alexandria where Strabo spent a number of years. Thus it is quite conceivable that a Jew, familiar with Greek and particularly Stoic philosophy, could have provided Strabo with the substance and perhaps even the actual form of his excursus on Moses. At the same time this hypothesis would explain how it is that elements of Hecataeus' earlier account seem to be present in Strabo, for we can safely assume that they would have been taken up, expanded, and embellished as part of a Hellenistic, perhaps apologetic Jewish theology.[72] Elements of Hecataeus' account of Moses may eventually have reached Strabo through such channels.

[67] Schürer, 3:156.
[68] Norden, "Jahve und Moses," p. 294.
[69] Nock, "Posidonius," p. 8.
[70] On these Hellenizers and their actions, see Tcherikover, *Hellenistic Civilization*, pp. 152-74.
[71] On Artapanus, cf. Eusebius, *Praep. Evang.* 9.27.1-6 (431a-432c) ; see also below, p. 77.
[72] From other references to Hecataeus within Hellenistic Judaism we know

Pompeius Trogus

In the case of Pompeius Trogus' *Historiae Philippicae* we are forced once again to depend on a later writer for our knowledge of the work.[73] Pompeius lived and wrote his history, known to have been composed in Latin, in the early reign of Augustus. Apart from the original prologues or tables of content, which have survived, and occasional references to Pompeius by later historians, our knowledge of Pompeius' *Histories* derives entirely from the later epitome of Justinus.[74]

The original prologue to book 36 includes these notices: "How Antiochus subdues the Jews, when Hyrcanus had been killed. Then, in a digression, the origins of the Jews are recalled." [75] Thus on the occasion of his first reference to the Jews, Pompeius inserted into the

---

that such a use was made of Hecataeus, i.e., the Ps-Hecataean writings of later times. Not all later references need be taken as Jewish works, although some of them surely are, e.g., the book on Abraham mentioned by Josephus, *AJ* 1.159. For discussions of Ps-Hecataeus, see Schürer, 3:603-8; B. Schaller, "Hekataios von Abdera über die Juden: Zur Frage der Echtheit und der Datierung," ZNW 54 (1963) : 15-31; and my article, "Pseudo-Hecataeus Again," ZNW 60 (1969) : 130-39.

[73] It is impossible to fix Pompeius' dates with precision. The firm chronological data are as follows: 38.3.11 refers to Livy's history and thus presupposes that at least a part of it had already been published, book 1 having been published not later than 25 B.C.E. The latest datable events in Pompeius' *Hist. Philip.* are the return of the Roman military standards to Augustus by the Parthians (42.5.11 = 20 B.C.E.) and the conclusion of Augustus' war in Spain (44.5.8 = 19 B.C.E.). On Pompeius' life and work, see A. Klotz, "Pompeius (14)," RE 42 (1952) : 2300 ff.; O. Seel, "Pompeius Trogus," in *Lexicon der alten Welt* (1965), pp. 2407 f.

[74] *M. Juniani Justini Epitoma Historiarum Philippicarum Pompei Trogi*, ed. O. Seel (1935). The date of Justinus is also problematic. In the absence of any information about him, scholars have settled on a date in the second or third centuries C.E. By comparing the topics mentioned in Pompeius' prologues with the material contained in Justinus' epitome, it is apparent, as Justinus himself admits, that he has eliminated a considerable bulk of Pompeius' materials: "I have selected what is most fitting for learning and omitted what is not agreeable to the joy of learning or essential to the contents *(exemplum)* ."

[75] *Pompeius Trogus Fragmenta*, ed. O. Seel (1956) p. 163. The Antiochus mentioned is Antiochus VII Sidetes (139/8-129), the son of Demetrius I Soter (162-150) . In 134 B.C.E. Antiochus VII besieged Hyrcanus, the son of Simon, in Jerusalem. Contrary to Pompeius' account which states that Antiochus subjugated the Jews after Hyrcanus' death, Josephus relates *(AJ* 13.236 ff.) that the siege ended in a happy alliance between Antiochus and Hyrcanus. According to Josephus, it was Simon, not his son Hyrcanus, who was killed just prior to Antiochus' invasion *(AJ* 13.228 f.) . It is not possible to determine whether the confusion should be attributed to Justinus, Pompeius, or one of Pompeius' sources, although Justinus is notorious for his unreliability concerning proper names; cf. Klotz, "Pompeius," p. 2304.

narrative a survey of Jewish origins (36.2.1-16). In so doing he was following his normal practice of presenting brief historical surveys whenever notable cities and peoples made their initial appearance in the narrative.[76]

(11) His [Joseph's] son was Moses whose physical beauty commended him as much as the wisdom which he inherited from his father.

(12) But when the Egyptians had been exposed to the scab and to a skin infection and had been warned by an oracle, they expelled him, together with the sick people, beyond the confines of Egypt lest the disease should spread to a greater number of people.

(13) Having been appointed leader of the exiles, he secretly took the holy objects of the Egyptians. In trying to recover these objects with force, the Egyptians were forced by storms to return home.

(14) Thus when Moses reached Damascus, his patriarchal homeland, he occupied Mount Sinai. When he finally arrived there with his people after seven days of hunger in the deserts of Arabia, he consecrated forever the seventh day, which is called Sabbata, according to the custom of the people, as a day of fast, because that day ended their hunger and wandering.

(15) And because they remembered that they had been expelled from Egypt due to fear of contagion, they took care not to live with outsiders lest they become hateful to the natives for the same reason [i.e., fear of contagious infection]. This regulation, which arose from a specific cause, he [Moses] transformed gradually into a fixed custom and religion.

(16) After Moses, his son Arruas was made a priest in the Egyptian rites and later king (*sacerdos sacris Aegyptiis, mox rex creatur*). Thereafter it has been the custom among the Jews to have the same persons as king and priest, as a result of whose uprightness, mixed with religion, the Jews have become amazingly powerful.

Pompeius' excursus on Jewish history is notable in several respects. Unlike other excurses which we have examined, Moses shares the central role with Joseph. Because his brothers envied his *excellens ingenium,* Joseph was sold into Egypt where he soon became a favorite of the king. The detailed description of Joseph's wisdom is worth quoting at length:

For he was highly skilled in prodigies and was the first to found the science of interpreting dreams. Nothing of divine or human law seemed to be un-

---

[76] Cf. 2.1 on the Scythians, 2.6 on Athens, 7.1 on Macedonia, 13.7 on Cyrene, 17.3 on Epirus, 18.3-7 on Carthage, 32.3 ff. on the Istrians and Docians, 42.2.7 ff. on Armenia, and 43.1 ff. on Italy.

known to him, so that he forecast a famine several years in advance, and all of Egypt would have perished if the king, on Joseph's advice, had not ordered grain to be stored for several years. So great were his proofs that his warnings seemed to be given by a god, not by a man.[77]

According to Pompeius' chronology, Moses was the son of Joseph. This contradicts the biblical genealogy according to which Moses descended from Levi. On the other hand, it agrees with the genealogy given by the Rhodian rhetor, Apollonius Molon, who refers to Moses as a descendant of Joseph (see above, p. 19). There is no compelling reason, however, to suppose a direct relationship between the two authors. A pagan writer might well be expected to assume a father-son relationship between the two leaders, for both belonged to the family of Jacob and the biblical narrative presents Moses as Joseph's successor as leader of the Israelites. One further reason for the confusion may lie in the portrayal of Moses' wisdom. Joseph is presented as a man of almost superhuman wisdom and learning, and Moses was already known among pagans as a man of great wisdom. Thus what could be more natural than to assume that Moses, whose credits were well established, derived his superlative wisdom from Joseph, a new figure in pagan literature, and that Joseph should become Moses' father?

The mention of Moses' physical beauty (*formae pulchritudo*) is an indication that Pompeius or his source was familiar with Jewish sources. Exod. 2:2 (LXX) describes the newborn Moses as "beautiful" (*asteion*). In similar fashion, Philo described Moses' appearance as "unusually beautiful" (*Mos.* 1.9), and Josephus states that Thermuthis, the daughter of the Egyptian king in Exod. 2:5, was amazed at Moses "because of his size and attractiveness" (*AJ* 2.224).

The second section deals with the expulsion and the exodus proper. Although the text does not explicitly identify the sick people in Egypt as Hebrews or Israelites, it clearly reflects the Alexandrian versions of the exodus in which the Jews are descended from exiled Egyptians.[78] As we have already seen, the earliest form of this expulsion tradition dates to the account of Hecataeus, where it applies to Greeks as well

[77] The main elements in this picture of Joseph correspond to the account in Gen. 37–41.
[78] At this point Pompeius' account seems somewhat confused. On the one hand he knows that the Jews are descendants of Abraham and Joseph and that their

as Jews. In the intervening period the tradition has undergone certain modifications and assumed something like a final form which appears in Manetho, Chaeremon, Lysimachus, Apion, and Tacitus (see below, pp. 113 ff.). The constant elements in the tradition are four in number: (1) the plague, (2) the expulsion itself, (3) the explanation of the expulsion in religious terms, sometimes in reference to oracular warnings, and (4) the leadership of Moses. These elements constitute the basic framework of the tradition in Hecataeus as well as Pompeius. The new elements in Pompeius are first that the tradition has now focused on the Jews alone as the objects of the expulsion; second, that the exiles themselves, not the Egyptians, are sick and impure; and third, that the cause of the plague is not foreign religious practice but rather the presence of impure people in the land of Egypt.[79]

In addition to these traditional elements, Pompeius' account includes a further incident which recalls the biblical narrative and perhaps also the exodus accounts of the Alexandrian anti-Jewish writers. The statement that Moses secretly took certain sacred objects (*sacra*) of the Egyptians echoes Exod. 12:35-36, which reports two items concerning the departing Israelites: first, that they requested and received from the Egyptians gold and silver vessels, and clothing; and second, that they plundered the Egyptians.[80] Philo, too, relates that the Jews took with them much spoil which, says Philo, was justifiable either as a peaceable payment for their labor or as a martial retaliation for their enslavement.[81]

Pompeius continues his narrative with the description of the Egyptians' unsuccessful attempt to recover their purloined religious objects. Their attempt was thwarted by storms, and they were forced to return to Egypt. Here again the narrative clearly presupposes some

---

ancient city of origin is Damascus (2.1 and 14), but he seems also to know the Alexandrian accounts in which the Jews derive from exiled Egyptians. His failure to reconcile these two traditions has led to the confusion in 2.12 where the exiles appear to be native Egyptians rather than the descendants of Joseph.

[79] Cf. Manetho, *apud* Josephus, *Ap.* 1.233, and Lysimachus, *ibid.* 1.306. Of these new elements, the first two arose from conflicts between Jews and Alexandrians subsequent to the time of Hecataeus. Cf. I. Heinemann, "Antisemitismus," RE Suppl. 5 (1931): 6 ff., and V. Tcherikover, *Hellenistic Civilization*, pp. 361 ff.

[80] The first statement is repeated in Josephus, *AJ* 2.314.

[81] *Mos.* 1.14 f. The theme of Jewish desecration of Egyptian temples appears also in the Alexandrian accounts of the exodus. Lysimachus even reports that the city of the Jews was originally called Hierosyla ("temple robbery") because of Jewish "sacrilegious propensities" (Josephus *Ap.* 1.311).

knowledge of the exodus story in Exod. 14:5-31. Pompeius' account diverges only in its brevity and its demythologized version of the miracle at the "Red Sea." As above, it is impossible to say whether the substitution of storms for the miraculous splitting of the sea was the work of a Jew or a pagan.

The account continues with the wanderings of the Jews in the Arabian deserts and their arrival at Damascus, their ancient fatherland: "when Moses reached Damascus, his patriarchal homeland, he occupied Mount Sinai." The identification of Damascus as the city of the Jews and the location of Sinai in Damascus is surprising. At the beginning of the excursus, Pompeius designates Damascus as the city of origin of the Jews (36.2.1). A few lines later he names Azelus, Adores, Abrahames, and Israhel as kings of Damascus.[82] A similar tradition is reflected by Nicolaus of Damascus. In book 4 of his *Histories,* as preserved by Josephus (*AJ* 1.159 f.), Nicolaus records that Abraham had ruled at Damascus, having come originally from the land of the Chaldaeans, and that his name was still (in Nicolaus' time) well known in the city. Although Pompeius either did not know or chose not to mention the Chaldaean origin of the Jews, we must presuppose common or related traditions behind Nicolaus and Pompeius. One might also ask whether this Damascene tradition reflects Jewish influence. It is certainly possible that Jews resident in Damascus, out of local patriotism, could have transferred not only Jewish origins but perhaps even the location of Mount Sinai to Damascus.[83] A second possibility is that the writer, in his ignorance of Palestinian geography, thought that Sinai was in fact located near Damascus. In either case, the reference to Sinai itself must stem from a Jewish source.

The third section is an attempt to relate the expulsion to various aspects of Jewish life (the sabbath, Jewish separatism, and the re-

[82] According to Reinach, *Textes,* p. 252, n. 1, Azelus represents Hazael, and Adores Hadad. The story of Hadad and Hazael is related in 1 Kings 8 and Josephus, *AJ* 9.87 ff.; cf. Freudenthal, *Hellenistische Studien,* p. 30, note.

[83] There is no direct evidence that later tradition located Sinai in Palestine or Syria. Ginzberg, *Legends of the Jews,* 6:32, n. 186, suggests that "the explanation of the word Moriah as the place where the teaching of God went forth . . . presupposes, perhaps, the legend that Sinai originally formed part of Moriah." In turn, Josephus (*AJ* 1.226) identifies Moriah with the temple-mount in Jerusalem. These tenuous bits of information merely suggest the possibility that Sinai's location was not irrevocably fixed in the peninsula.

ligious system of the Jews). According to Pompeius, the sabbath was a day of fasting in commemoration of the fact that the Jews arrived in their homeland after seven days of hunger in the deserts of Arabia.[84] Apart from reminiscences of the exodus account (the hunger of the people in Exod. 16:3 and the wandering in the desert in Exod. 14 ff.), there are two additional elements in the explanation of the sabbath. The first is the understanding of the sabbath as a day of fast. This (mis-) understanding was widespread in antiquity, especially among authors associated with Rome. It was shared by Strabo (16.2. 40), the Emperor Augustus,[85] and the poet Martial (*Epigr.* 4.4), and Petronius (Fr. 37 Bücheler). On the other hand, Agatharchides of Cnidus (*apud* Josephus, *Ap.* 1.209), Apion (*ibid.* 2.21), and Tacitus (*Hist.* 5.4) correctly report the sabbath as a day of rest and make no mention of fasting.

The second new element is the explanation of sabbath's origin. Moses set apart the seventh day, says Pompeius, because on it the Jews ended their seven days in the desert. In the Jewish scriptures there are two distinct aetiologies of the sabbath. One stems from the seven days of creation (Gen. 2:3; Exod. 20:11), while the other is based on the events of the exodus (Deut. 5:15). Thus it would appear that Pompeius' explanation of the origin of the sabbath also derives from Jewish sources. This conclusion receives further support from Tacitus who refers his explanation to the Jews themselves: "They say that they chose the seventh day for rest because that day brought an end to their labors (*Hist.* 5.4).

Following his explanation of the sabbath, Pompeius proceeds to the phenomenon of Jewish separatism, i.e., their refusal to live with foreigners. It is interesting that he presupposes this separatism as a well-known fact and presents it with no undertones of reproach or hostility. Once again, Pompeius uses the exodus to explain the origin of a Jewish practice. Their separatism is presented as a defensive reaction to the fact that they had been expelled by the Egyptians from fear of contagion. Thus rather than risk further hostility and rejection by their new neighbors, the Jews resolved to live apart from them.[86]

[84] Unlike other writers, Pompeius offers no etymological explanation of the term "sabbath."

[85] Suetonius, *Aug.* 76: "Not even a Jew, dear Tiberius, has observed the sabbath fast as diligently as I have observed it today."

[86] Essentially the same explanation as that given by Hecataeus. The attitude of

The section on the origins of Jewish religion concludes with the observation that Moses gradually transformed this historically conditioned reaction into a fixed element of a religious system. In presenting Moses as the founder of the Israelite religion, it simply summarizes the preceding statements to the effect that given religious practices took their origins in specific historical events.

The Moses material concludes with the statement that Arruas (= Aaron) succeeded Moses as priest of the Egyptian holy rites and soon thereafter was appointed king. As in the case of Joseph and Moses, so here a father-son relationship apparently is established between Moses and Aaron.[87] At the same time, the tradition of Moses as an Egyptian priest has been transferred to Aaron, although Pompeius does not state explicitly that Moses himself was a priest. As it stands, 2.16 seems to say that Aaron succeeded Moses in the Egyptian rites which were set up in Jerusalem. However, this may be another instance of Pompeius' failure or inability to digest diverse strands of information, i.e., Moses is an Egyptian priest according to certain Alexandrian writers, and Aaron a priest of Israel in the Jewish tradition.[88] 2.16 then concludes with the rather remarkable comment that the uprightness (*iustitia*) and religion (*religio,* not *superstitio*) of their rulers have led the Jews to a point of considerable (*incredibile quantum*) power. In conformity with the regular pattern of such excursus on the Jews, the historical excursus is then followed by a description of certain physical characteristics of Palestine and a brief summary of the various foreign powers who later ruled over the Jews (36.3.1-9).

What, then, of Pompeius' attitude toward Moses? One critic has designated the passage as one of the many hostile accounts of the

---

amixia was a common reproach directed against the Jews; cf. the Emperor Claudius (*apud* Josephus, *AJ* 19.290) who enjoins them "not to set at nought the beliefs about the gods held by other people." The extent to which this criticism influenced the thinking of Jews may be seen in the reaction of the "Hellenizers" in 1 Macc. 1:11 (". . . for since we separated from them, i.e., the Gentiles, many evils have come upon us"). Philo also bears direct witness to Jewish sensitivity on this point: "Therefore it strikes me as amazing that some people dare to accuse the people, i.e., the Jews, of inhumanity (*apanthropia*) " (*Spec. leg.* 2.167).

[87] In Exod. 6:20 Aaron is Moses' brother.

[88] The only possible parallel to the notion that Moses set up an Egyptian-type cult in Jerusalem is the account of Apion, on whom see below, pp. 122 ff.

Jews.[89] There is little in Pompeius' account to justify such a claim. Joseph and Moses receive unqualified praise as men of superior wisdom. The account of the expulsion, which of itself is unsympathetic toward the Jews, is related in the simplest possible manner and hardly reflects the familiar Egyptian point of view. The picture of Jewish religion, including the aspect of separatism, lacks entirely the bitter hostility of other writers. Finally, the concluding sentence ascribes the political success of the Jews to the justice and religion of their priest-kings. On the whole, the passage reflects a positive rather than a negative, or even a neutral attitude toward Moses as a figure of Jewish history and toward the Jews in general.

In our analysis of Pompeius we have seen that a variety of elements contributed to the final form of the excursus on Moses and the Jews. These elements include the biblical account of the exodus or, as seems more likely, a later Jewish account of the same; a local Damascene tradition which located the origin of the Jews in Damascus; and a modified Egyptian account of the exodus similar to the versions of the Alexandrians and Tacitus. The question is whether Pompeius himself collected the various elements and composed the excursus, or whether he took it over from an earlier writer in substantially its present form. If we keep in mind that Pompeius was writing a universal history from the time of the Assyrians under King Ninus to the time of Augustus, it would seem most reasonable to assume that he relied on one main source for each successive period of his history. Not surprisingly, the name of Poseidonius has been proposed by several critics.[90]

J. Morr has argued that the descriptions of Palestine in Strabo (16.2.41-44), Josephus (*BJ* 4.459-485), Pompeius, and Tacitus (*Hist.* 5.6-7) all derive directly or indirectly from Poseidonius.[91] His evidence is that all the accounts follow a common outline: the historical excursus, the balsams of Jericho, the asphalt of the Dead Sea, and finally, Sodom. But when we compare the descriptions given by Strabo and

---

[89] J. Morr, "Die Landeskunde von Palästina bei Strabon und Josephus," *Philologus* 81 (1925): 278.

[90] In addition, Schürer, 1:52 f., proposed Nicolaus of Damascus, while Jacoby (FGH 2C:220 f.) and others have suggested Timagenes of Alexandria; for an assessment of the Timagenes suggestion, see A. Lesky, *A History of Greek Literature* (ET 1966), p. 778.

[91] Morr, "Landeskunde," pp. 256 ff.

Pompeius, the two accounts have little in common. The only general point of comparison is the description of the plain of Jericho. Even here, however, the details of Strabo's account cannot be reconciled with those of Pompeius. Thus, if Strabo relied primarily on Poseidonius in his description of Palestine, it cannot be maintained reasonably that Pompeius used the same source. The only method of salvaging the argument would be to affirm that Strabo derived this information from Poseidonius' *On the Ocean*[92] whereas Pompeius used his *Histories*, and that Justinus has seriously condensed Pompeius' account, or that Pompeius took his historical information from Poseidonius and his geographical description from some other source. At this point, however, the chain of assumptions shows definite signs of weakness, and the argument begins to look like another case of *horror vacui.*

This much can be said with certainty. As a totality, the excursus derives from none of the extant writings on the Jews. Thus we are left with something of a vacuum concerning Pompeius' immediate source. As to its pre-Pompeian development, we should probably see the excursus as having passed through several stages: first, a Jewish source from which the information about Joseph and Moses was derived; second, a Damascene source, including Jewish elements, which identified Damascus as the metropolis of the Jews; and finally, a pagan source which included the traditional account of the expulsion of the sick people from Egypt under the leadership of Moses. The presence of these elements is certain; the order, manner, and place of their integration are uncertain.

"Longinus"

Few passages in post-classical Greek literature have received as much attention as the so-called Genesis quotation in "Longinus," *On the Sublime.*[93] In response to a request from his patron, "Longinus"

[92] So Reinhardt, *Ursprung,* p. 71.
[93] *"Longinus," On the Sublime,* edited with introduction and commentary by D. A. Russell (1964). The author of the treatise is unknown. In his discussion of date and authorship (xxii-xxx), Russell leans toward a date in the first century c.e. In the earliest manuscript (Parisinus 2036), from which all other manuscripts descend, the author is identified as "Dionysios Longinos" in the title, and "Dionysios ē Longinos" in the table of contents. It is generally agreed that both forms represent scribal attempts to assign an author to the treatise. "Dionysios" probably

56

composed this essay on elevated or sublime style for his patron's personal use.[94] The bulk of the essay is devoted to a discussion of the five sources of elevated style, the first and most important of which is greatness of mind.[95] For "Longinus" the basic element of great writing is not literary style proper but rather a noble and elevated mind. "Great writing," he states "is the echo of a great mind" (9.2).

As examples of this greatness of mind, he cites the silence of Ajax in *Odyssey* 11.543-567; a verbal exchange between Alexander and Parmenio;[96] three further passages from Homer, and finally the passage from Genesis. The first of the three Homer passages, *Iliad* 5.770, is cited with approval as "magnifying the heavenly beings." The second passage, a conflation of theomachies from *Iliad* 21.388 and 20.61-65, is praised for its literary merits but blamed as "utterly impious and without regard for what is proper," i.e., concerning the gods.[97] The third passage, a conflation of *Iliad* 13.18, 20.60, 13.19, and 13.27-29, is contrasted with the theomachies and lauded for its presentation of the deity as "unalloyed" (*achranton*), elevated (*mega*), and pure (*akraton*). As a final example of a noble conception of the deity he cites the Genesis passage:

In the same manner, what does the lawgiver (*thesmothetēs*) of the Jews say (*phēsi*)—no ordinary man, for he comprehended and brought to light

---

refers to Dionysius of Halicarnassus (*fl.* 30-8 B.C.E.), and "Longinos" to the third-century C.E. rhetor and friend of Porphyry, Cassius Longinus.

[94] The essay was written in part as a reply to a certain Caecilius who had published an earlier treatise, *Peri Hypsous*. The Caecilius in question is undoubtedly Caecilius of Calacte in Sicily. The Suidas notice on Caecilius reads as follows: "Rhetor . . . in the time of Caesar Augustus down to the time of Hadrian, born of slaves . . . he was first known as Archagathos, and in his *doxa* he was Jewish." Caecilius, then, was at least a Jewish sympathizer, if not a proselyte or even a Jew by birth. On Caecilius, see Th. Reinach, "Quid Judaeo cum Verre?" REJ 26 (1893): 36-46; W. Rhys Roberts, "Caecilius of Calacte," AJP 18 (1897): 302-12; Brzoska, "Caecilius (2)," RE 5 (1899): 1174-88; and Russell, pp. 58 f.

[95] *To megalophyes*. But "Longinus" is not consistent in identifying and naming this source—in 8 he calls it *to peri tas noēseis adrepēbolon*, and in the conclusion of this first section (15.12) it is *ta kata noēseis hypsēla*.

[96] The contents of this exchange are lacking due to the loss of six MS pages. Arrian, *Anab.* 2.25.2, however, records the exchange as follows: "Parmenio . . . affirmed that were he Alexander he would close with these terms and stop the war without further risks; then Alexander answered Parmenio that he would indeed have done this were he Parmenio. . . ."

[97] H. Mutschmann, "Das Genesiscitat in der Schrift ΠΕΡΙ ΥΨΟΥΣ," *Hermes* 52 (1917): 167, and G. Grube, "Notes on the ΠΕΡΙ ΥΨΟΥΣ," AJP 78 (1957): 365 f.

in worthy fashion the power of the deity—when he wrote at the very beginning of the laws, "God said, 'Let there be light!' and there was; 'Let there be earth!' and there was"? (9.9) [98]

"Longinus' " introduction of a reference to Moses at this point and in such positive terms has caused some scholars considerable anguish. For many, the obvious solution was to reject the lines as a Jewish or Christian interpolation.[99] This position was thoroughly examined and rejected by H. Mutschmann in 1917, and since his time the question has hardly been raised again.[100] Mutschmann argued not only that the passage belongs in its present context but that it was the very capstone of "Longinus' " argument.[101] A somewhat different view has been argued by E. Norden,[102] who attempted to show that 9.6-9 (the criticism of Homer's theology and the Genesis passage) was inserted by "Longinus" from a separate source and that the criticism of Homer's theology cannot be reconciled with the praise of the *Iliad* in 9.3 and 13.[103]

Concerning Norden's first observation, it should be noted that the section in question consists of a series of passages which are alternately criticized and praised, and that the criticism of the Homeric theomachies fits this pattern neatly.

The terms used to introduce Moses confirm the view that "Longinus" regarded him as at least Homer's equal in matters concerning the

[98] The complex word order of the passage has given rise to slight variations in translation. The main issue is whether the subject of *phēsi* is Moses or the deity. Russell (93), and E. Norden, *Das Genesiszitat in der Schrift vom Erhabenen* (1955), pp. 18 f. agree that the subject is Moses. Russell translates (93): "A similar effect was achieved by the lawgiver of the Jews—no mean genius, for he both understood and gave expression to the power of the divinity as it deserved—when he wrote at the very beginning of his laws—I quote his words—'God said'—what? —'Let there be light.' And there was. 'Let there be earth.' And there was."

[99] The classic example of this approach is K. Ziegler's article, "Das Genesiscitat in der Schrift ΠΕΡΙ ΥΨΟΥΣ," *Hermes* 50 (1915): 572-603. His basic argument was that the parallels in thought and vocabulary with Jewish writings could not possibly stem from "Longinus" himself and that the Genesis passage itself broke the train of "Longinus' " thought.

[100] Mutschmann, "Genesiscitat," pp. 161 ff.

[101] *Ibid.*, p. 171: "Von seiner Weltanschauung aus betrachtet ist das Genesiscitat bei weitem erhabener und grossartiger als jene Stelle Homers."

[102] Norden, *Genesiszitat*, pp. 5 ff.

[103] "Longinus" contrasts the *Iliad* and the *Odyssey* as follows: "It was for this reason, I imagine, that, writing the *Iliad* at the acme of his genius he made the whole piece dramatic and engaging, whereas the *Odyssey* is mostly narrative, which is a sign of old age."

gods. "Longinus" is the first author, whether pagan, Jewish, or Christian, to use the archaic *thesmothetēs* of Moses.[104] We should probably assume that, taken with the following appositional phrase "no ordinary man," the choice of *thesmothetēs* represents a deliberate attempt by the author to underline Moses' theological excellence. The ground for this judgment is then spelled out in the following clause: "for he comprehended and brought to light in worthy fashion the power of the deity. . . ." In line with his theory that great style necessarily presupposes great ideas, especially in matters concerning the gods, "Longinus" praises the deity as one whose power was so great that his word alone was sufficient for creation.[105]

As for the passage from Moses, "Longinus" notes correctly that it occurs at the very beginning of Moses' laws. In fact it seems to be an isocolonic paraphrase of Gen. 1:3 and 1:9-10 (LXX); the texts compare as follows:

"Longinus"	*Genesis 1:3, 9-10*
εἶπεν ὁ θεός.	καὶ εἶπεν ὁ θεός
γενέσθω φῶς,	γενηθήτω φῶς.
καὶ ἐγένετο.	καὶ ἐγένετο φῶς. . . .
	καὶ εἶπεν ὁ θεός . . .
γενέσθω γῆ,	ὀφθήτω ἡ ξηρά.
καὶ ἐγένετο.	καὶ ἐγένετο οὕτως.
	. . . καὶ ἐκάλεσαν ὁ θεὸς τὴν ξηρὰν γῆν . . . .

In its present form the "quotation" is probably "Longinus'" careful rephrasing of the Genesis material.[106] Just as he regularly rephrased and conflated passages from Homer and Plato, so he also altered the verses from Genesis to suit his own stylistic purposes.

[104] Winnifried Bühler, *Beiträge zur Erklärung der Schrift vom Erhabenen* (1964), notes that *thesmothetēs* normally designates the so-called junior archons of Athens, and that *thesmos* often indicates divine as opposed to human legislation (34).

[105] In his commentary on 9.9, Russell cites the eleventh-century rhetor, John of Sicily, who offers the following comments on our passage: "The best not only among Christians but also among Greeks, including Longinus and Demetrius of Phalerum, revere him [Moses] highly" (6.211).

[106] So Mutschmann, "Genesiscitat," pp. 173 f. It is of no real significance that the version of Aquila (*ca.* 130 C.E.) also reads *genesthō* in Gen. 1:3, since "Longinus'" version otherwise diverges as much from Aquila as it does from LXX.

The Problem of "Longinus'" Source

Attempts to determine the source of "Longinus'" Genesis "quotation" have led to three widely divergent solutions. Apart from the purely negative solution which rejects the passage as a later interpolation, the two remaining proposals have been that "Longinus" himself was a Jew of some sort or that he was a pagan Greek who knew and used Jewish sources. In both cases the body of evidence is essentially the same.

The first bit of evidence is the form of the Genesis passage. Russell has suggested that the free quotation tells against the possibility of direct Jewish authorship.[107] While it is generally true that Jewish and Christian writers quote Jewish scriptures with reasonable, if not infallible, accuracy, we should recall that earlier Jewish apologists did not hesitate to reshape and restate the scriptures almost at will. Furthermore, the character of the treatise and its author—if indeed he be Jewish—is of such a nature that early Christian writers and even Philo cannot be cited as authoritative parallels. Thus we should not put undue emphasis on the form of the "quotation" as evidence for or against the possibility of Jewish authorship.

Of greater interest are a number of parallels between "Longinus" and Jewish writings of the same time. Norden has pointed out that the active use of *chōrein* with the accusative, while rare in pagan literature, occurs some twenty-five times in Philo and is generally limited to Jewish and Christian writings.[108] Furthermore, passages in the preface of Josephus' *Antiquities* bear a close resemblance to "Longinus" 9. The first, *AJ* 1.15, recalls "Longinus" 9.9:

Josephus	"Longinus"
I entreat those who will read these volumes . . .	
to test whether our lawgiver has had a *worthy conception of His nature* and has always assigned to Him such *actions as befit His power*, keeping his words concerning Him pure	For he, i.e. Moses, *comprehended* and brought to light in *worthy fashion* the *power* of the deity.

[107] Russell, p. 93.
[108] For parallels in Philo, cf. *Det.* 89 f. and *Praem.* 39.

of that unseemly mythology
current among others. . . .

The second, *AJ* 1.22, recalls "Longinus" 9.7:

Josephus	*"Longinus"*
Other legislators, following fables, have in their writings imputed to the gods the disgraceful errors of men . . . our legislator, on the contrary, having shown that God possesses the very perfection of virtue. . . .	I feel that in recording as he does *the wounding of the gods, their quarrels, vengeance, tears, imprisonment, and all their manifold passions* Homer has done his best to make the men in the *Iliad* gods and the gods men.

Finally Norden calls attention to the speech of the philosopher in 44.
He isolates four main themes in the speech: the rarity of outstanding
men among the philsopher's contemporaries; the assertion that great
literature is possible only in a democracy; the observation that only
free men, not slaves, can produce great writing; and the idea that
custom and habit are powerful forces among humans. These four
ideas, says Norden, are also basic to the thought of Philo of Alexandria.[109]

This parallel between Philo and the philosopher is further strength-
ened by certain verbal similarities between 44.3-4 and Philo *Ebr.* 198:

"Longinus"	*Philo*
In our own day, . . . we learn unjust slavery as children, we are all but swaddled (*monon ouk enesparganōmenoi*) in its customs . . . ; no slave ever becomes an orator, for immediately the inability to speak and the feeling of	Now I do not wonder that the chaotic and promiscuous multitude who are bound in glorious slavery to usages and customs introduced in whatever manner, and who are indoctrinated from the cradle (*ap' autōn eti sparganōn*) with the lesson of

[109] *Genesiszitat* 17: "Es gibt . . . in der ganzen Rede des 'Philosophen' bei dem Anonymus auch nicht einen führenden Gedanken, der sich uns nicht als philonisch erwiesen hätte. . . ."

imprisonment which has been regularly beaten into him through habit (*hypo sunētheias aei kekondulismenou*) . . . .

obedience to them, as to masters and despots, with their souls buffeted into subjection (*katakekondulismenos tēn psychēn*) and incapable of entertaining any high or generous feeling, should give credence to traditions delivered once for all . . . .

Such is the evidence. From it Norden has concluded that "Longinus" was a pagan Greek author who knew and used Jewish writings, especially those of Philo. Specifically, he proposes that "Longinus" met and talked with Philo during the latter's embassy to the Emperor Gaius in 40 C.E. Gaius' death in 41, the ensuing political debates about the fortunes of democracy, the happy reversal of Jewish fortunes under Claudius, and the prominence of Philo's own family would have provided ideal conditions for such an encounter. Beyond this, Norden suggests that "Longinus" may have known Philo's writings and taken the Genesis quotation from Philo's lost *Apology*.

A different solution, proposed variously by Th. Mommsen, W. Christ, W. B. Sedgwick, and Russell, is that "Longinus" himself was a hellenized Jew. [110] This solution avoids the difficulty of making the already hypothetical meeting of "Longinus" and Philo dependent on the admittedly tenuous dating of "Longinus" himself. It accounts for the fact that parallels with Philo appear not only in the philosopher's speech but at other places as well. Rather than positing a direct Philonic influence throughout the writing, G. Goold suggests that it makes better sense to assume that "Longinus" belonged to the same environment which produced Philo and that he "is in some sense a Jew." [111] There are in fact no religious, philosophical, or

---

[110] Mommsen, *Römische Geschichte* (1885) 5:494: "Die Abhandlung . . . rührt sicher wenn nicht von einem Juden, so doch von einem Mann her, der Homeros und Moses gleichmässig verehrte." Christ, *Geschichte der griechischen Literatur*[4] (1905) : 788: ". . . Wahrscheinlich war er ein hellenischer Jude." Sedgwick, "Sappho in 'Longinus' (X,2, Line 13) ," AJP 69 (1948) : 198 f. and tentatively, Russell, xxx: "Mommsen thought that L was a Hellenized Jew; this cannot be proved, but it cannot be disproved either."

[111] "A Greek Professorial Circle at Rome," TAPA 92 (1961) : 177.

literary objections to this hypothesis. That "Longinus' " basic cultural sympathies lay in the tradition of the Greek classics is obvious. This is, however, no argument against calling him a Jew or a Jewish sympathizer. As we shall see presently in the case of Numenius of Apamea (below, pp. 68 f.), the line of demarcation between Greeks with Jewish sympathies and hellenized Jews could be extremely vague in cultural, philosophical and religious matters. Thus it may be little more than a matter of personal preference whether we call "Longinus" a thoroughly hellenized Jew or a pagan with knowledge of and sympathy for aspects of hellenized Judaism.

Numenius of Apamea

In moving from "Longinus" in the first or second century C.E. to Numenius in the middle of the second century C.E., we are still in hotly disputed and uncertain territory. Of Numenius' life we know only that his home city was Apamea on the Orontes in Syria, that he was known as both a Platonic and a Pythagorean philosopher, and that his writings, of which only fragments survive,[112] exerted considerable influence within later Neoplatonism.

In line with the fascination of nascent Neoplatonism for the wisdom of the East, Numenius occasionally appeals to non-Greek sources in support of his own ideas:

When one has spoken of this and confirmed it with the testimonies of Plato, it will be necessary to return and relate it to the teachings of Pythagoras and finally to call upon the outstanding nations, bringing in the rites and doctrines and institutions which the Brahmans, the Jews, the Magi and the Egyptians established and founded in agreement with Plato.[113]

---

[112] The standard critical edition of Numenius' fragments is E. A. Leemans, *Studie over den Wijsgeer Numenius van Apamea met Uitgave der Fragmenten* (1937). All references to Numenius will be given according to Leemans' enumeration of the testimonia (T.) and the fragments (Fr.). Cf. also the older and very incomplete edition, with translation, of K. S. Guthrie, *Numenius of Apamea. The Father of Neo-Platonism* (1917). On Numenius, see also R. Beutler, "Numenius," RE Suppl. 7 (1950): 664-78; H.-C. Puech, "Numénius d'Apamée et les théologies orientales au second siècle," in *Mélanges Bidez* 2 (1934): 745-78; E. R. Dodds, "Numenius and Ammonius," in *Les sources de Plotin* (1960), pp. 3-32; and J. H. Waszink, "Porphyrios und Numenios," in *Porphyre* (1966), pp. 35-78.

[113] Fr. 9a = Eusebius, *Praep. Evang.* 9.7.1 (411c).

63

This statement, which appears in the first book of his *On the Good,* represents a programmatic attempt to include and incorporate the wisdom of certain non-Greek peoples into an essentially Platonic system of thought. His method seems to have been to examine those aspects of their thought which agreed or could be made to agree with Plato with a view to citing them as further authorities for his own point of view.[114] Within this system, Moses and the Jews occupied an important position. Origen indicates quite clearly that Numenius' method was to harmonzie Jewish scripture with Greek philosophy by means of allegory:

I am also aware that Numenius the Pythagorean, a man who expounded Plato with very great skill and maintained the Pythagorean doctrines, quotes Moses and the prophets in many passages and gives them no improbable allegorical interpretation, as in the writing called *Epops,* in his *On Numbers* and in his *On the Place.*[115]

According to Origen, Numenius interpreted "Moses and the prophets." This may represent something of an exaggeration by Origen in an effort to magnify the Jewish scriptures through the authority of Numenius, for there is direct evidence only that he used the book of Genesis. We do know, however, that he mentioned the Jews in connection with nations who "believe god to be incorporeal" (Fr. 9b) [116] and that he regarded the god of the Jews as "incompatible (*akoinōnētos*)," presumably with other deities, and as "the father of all gods, who deemed it unfitting that any one should share his honor with him." [117] Thus, while there is no direct evidence that he quoted writings outside the Pentateuch, the probability is that he did. However that may be, there seems little doubt that Moses was his chief authority and point of interest. Two fragments have survived which attest his importance for Numenius.

[114] For other examples of this argument in Middle Platonism, an argument from the *consensus gentium,* see Festugière, *Révélation,* 4:109 f.

[115] Fr. 7 = Origen, *c. Cels.* 4.51.

[116] Fr. 9b = *c. Cels.* 1.15; on the incorporeality of god in Middle Platonism, see Festugière, *Révélation,* 4:136.

[117] Fr. 34 = Lydus, *Mens.* 4.53. Behind these statements is probably the commandment in Exod. 20:3: "You shall have no other gods before me"; cf. 20:5: "for I the Lord your God am a jealous God."

We [Porphyry] say that the Naiads are nymphs and in particular the powers which preside over the waters; they [the theologians] use the term generally of all souls that descend into generation. For they consider, as Numenius says, that the souls rest on divinely blown water; therefore, he says, the prophet said that the spirit of god was borne over the water.[118]

In his allegorical writing, De Antro Nympharum, Porphyry attempts to discover the hidden meaning in Homer's cave of the Naiad nymphs (Odyssey 13.102-12). The cave or grotto, he says, is commonly a symbol of the material world, of the hidden forces in nature, and of intelligible reality. This particular cave, dedicated to the Naiad water nymphs, symbolizes intelligible reality bound to matter (hē enylos ousia). Theologians, he continues, apply the term Naiad generally to the nymphs or powers which rule over the waters and specifically to all souls as they enter into the process of birth and generation.

In this connection, Numenius, whom Porphyry cites as one of the theologians who had allegorized the Naiad cave, introduced a quotation by "the prophet" concerning the divine spirit which was borne over the waters. The prophet in question is obviously Moses. The reference is to Gen. 1:2 (LXX), pneuma theou epephereto epanō tou hydatos.[119] It is difficult to determine how Numenius used this quotation, for Porphyry gives no indication either of its original context or of the particular writing in which it occurred. Even in its present context the meaning is by no means clear. Does pneuma refer to the fact that the water was divinely blown,[120] or to the powers that rule over the waters, or to the descent of souls into birth? Porphyry's

[118] T. 46 = Porphyry, De Antro Nymph. 10: Νύμφας δὲ ναίδας λέγομεν καὶ τὰς τῶν ὑδάτων προεστώσας δυνάμεις ἰδίως, ἔλεγον δὲ καὶ τὰς εἰς γένεσιν κατιούσας ψυχὰς κοινῶς ἀπάσας. ἡγοῦντο γὰρ προσιζάνειν τῷ ὕδατι τὰς ψυχὰς θεοπνόῳ ὄντι, ὥς φησιν ὁ Νουμήνιος, διὰ τοῦτο λέγων καὶ τὸν προφήτην εἰρηκέναι ἐμφέρεσθαι ἐπάνω τοῦ ὕδατος θεοῦ πνεῦμα.

[119] The only divergence from the LXX is the prefix em, which is unparalleled in the apparatus to the LXX. It is quite possible that it represents Numenius' own stylistic alteration of the LXX text.

[120] The meaning of theopnous is somewhat ambiguous. In the Corp. Herm. 1.30 the speaker describes himself as theopnous genomenos tēs alētheias after hearing the mysterious discourse of the great Poimandres. Festugière's translation (Corpus Hermeticum 1:17), "rempli du souffle divin de la vérité," retains the literal meaning of the two components in theo-pnous. In our case the literal sense should also be retained and the term understood as expressing the effect of the divine breath on the water's surface.

reasoning runs as follows: (1) Numenius is among those who believed that the Naiads designated souls descending into birth and that souls rested on (the) water which was divinely blown; (2) in support of his view Numenius quoted a passage from the prophet Moses. In other words, Porphyry is reporting Numenius' views, not his own. The key seems to be the verbal connection between the *theopnous* in Numenius' system and the *pneuma theou* of Gen. 1:2. Thus Numenius interpreted *pneuma theou* in one of two ways: either the *pneuma* represents the souls themselves as they rest on the water, or, more probably, the spirit borne over the water explains how and why the water was *theopnous*. In either case, we learn from Porphyry that Numenius, in accordance with his methodological statement in his *On the Good,* cited Moses as an authority for some aspect of his philosophical system concerning the origin of the soul.

The second pertinent passage first appears in Clement of Alexandria (d. *ca.* 215 c.e.). In keeping with his belief in the barbarian origins of Greek philosophy, Clement quotes from the Jewish apologist Aristobulus: "and even Plato followed our legislation" (*Strom.* 1.[22.]150.1). As further testimony to Plato's dependence on Jewish wisdom, he cites the saying of Numenius, prefixing his own introduction: "Numenius the Phythagorean philosopher says clearly, 'What is Plato but Moses speaking Attic?'" (*ti gar esti Platōn ē Mōusēs attikizōn;* Fr. 10=*Strom.* 1.[22.]150.4). The next occurrence is in Eusebius' *Praeparatio Evangelica* (*ca.* 315-20 c.e.). The saying occurs first in 9.6.9 (411a), in a direct quotation from the passage of Clement discussed above, although unlike Clement, Eusebius uses it to demonstrate that pagan writers knew the history and philosophy of the Jews. The second occurrence is in 11.10.14 (527a), where Eusebius demonstrates in detail the harmony between Greek philosophy, especially Plato, and the Hebrew oracles. After a long excerpt from Numenius' *On the Good* he concludes as follows: "Rightly then is the saying attributed to him [Numenius] in which he is reported to have said, 'What is Plato etc.'" Following Eusebius, the saying next appears in book 2 of Theodoret's *Graecarum Affectionum Curatio* (*ca.* 430 c.e.), where it seems to be quoted from Eusebius.[121] Theodoret's use of the

[121] *Graec. Affect. Cur.* 2.114 f. (p. 67 ed. Raeder). Just prior to this passage, in 2.97, Theodoret refers the reader to Eusebius' *Praeparatio Evangelica* for further information about the stupidity of pagan myths.

saying is essentially the same as Clement's and Eusebius' in that it reaffirms Plato's dependence on Hebrew wisdom. Only in one respect does he move beyond the earlier formulation: "With these remarks Numenius openly proves that whatever Plato said that was of any value, he stole (sesylēken) from the theology of Moses." With the addition of sylan, Theodoret has changed the tone of the saying by making of Plato a plunderer rather than a mere borrower. From Theodoret the saying found its way into the chronicle of the sixth-century historian, Hesychius of Miletus:[122]

Numenius the Apamean, a Pythagorean philosopher, questioned the thought of Plato, because he stole what he said about god and the cosmos from the books of Moses. Therefore he [Numenius] said, "What is Plato etc."

Finally, Suidas (ca. 1000 C.E.) copied Hesychius, almost word for word, thus marking the final stage in the history of the saying:

Numenius: an Apamean from Syria and a Pythagorean philosopher. He questioned the thought of Plato, because he stole what he said about god and the generation of the cosmos from the Mosaic (books); for this reason he [Numenius] said, "What is Plato etc." (Suidas, s.v. Noumēnios.)

The question is whether to regard the saying as an authentic statement of Numenius. The first problem is the formulation itself, about which Dodds has the following to say: "If it were safe to generalize from this single example (our only one), we might urge that instead of describing Plato as 'Moses talking Attic' Numenius ought to have described Moses as 'Plato talking Hebrew.'" [123] In fact, as Dodds correctly observes, the saying is formulated from a Jewish rather than a Greek point of view. Moses is the primary figure and Plato is said to be like him. This formulation has led some to reject the saying as a Jewish creation.[124] If we rely on the evidence of Clement and Eusebius alone, our conclusion must be somewhat different. Clement, who lived not more and probably less than fifty years after Numenius,

---

[122] *Fragmenta Historicorum Graecorum*, ed. C. Müller, 4 (1885): 171.
[123] Dodds, "Numenius and Ammonius," p. 6 (emphasis Dodds').
[124] Reinach, *Textes*, p. 175, n. 2; cf. the somewhat different view of Schürer, 3:627: "Der Ausspruch ist also nicht eine jüdische Fälschung, sondern nur eine der mündlichen Ueberlieferung angehörige Zuspitzung der wirklichen Anschauung des Numenius."

cites it as an authentic saying with no signs of hesitation. The case of Eusebius is somewhat more complicated. In *Praep. Evang.* 9.6.9 (411a) he simply repeats Clement's version, but in 11.10.14 (527a) he seems less certain of its authenticity, although he recognizes that it is appropriate as a description of Numenius' dependence on Moses. The reason for Eusebius' apparent reluctance is not clear. Did some of his contemporaries question its authenticity? Did he doubt it himself or change his mind after writing 9.6? We can only say that Eusebius' testimony is curiously ambivalent. Beyond this we can affirm that Clement outweighs Eusebius simply because of his chronological proximity to Numenius, that Eusebius himself admits that the attribution makes good sense, and that there is no compelling reason to deny the authenticity of the saying.[125]

Can we move one step further and claim, as some have, that Numenius was a Jew? [126] As for the name, it is attested within Judaism. It appears in 1 Macc. 12:16 as the name of an ambassador to Rome under the reign of Jonathan (*ca.* 160 B.C.E.). In addition, the name *Noumēnis* appears on three Jewish tomb inscriptions at Rome.[127] The problem, however, concerns more than onomastics. The issue is whether a Jew could have written that Yahweh was the father of all the gods (Fr. 34), that the Egyptians were the equal of the Jews in knowledge of the gods (Fr. 9a), and that Jannes and Jambres (see below, pp. 139 f.) could have matched Moses in a contest of magic (Fr. 18). Obviously such a Jew would have been "very unorthodox" indeed.[128] But we have already noted that preconceived notions of what constituted orthodoxy in post-exilic Judaism are of little help in such matters. The existence, apparently unnoticed, of Jews like Artapanus and the Hellenizers in 1 Macc. 1 and 2 Macc. 4 makes it impossible for any critic to assert that Numenius could not

---

[125] So Puech, *Mélanges*, 2:753 f., and, apparently, Dodds, "Numenius and Ammonius," p. 6. I take Dodds's silence on this particular issue as evidence that he accepts the authenticity of the saying.

[126] So C. Bigg, *The Christian Platonists of Alexandria* (1913 ²), p. 300, n. 1., and Puech, *Mélanges*, 2:754: "S'il n'est donc pas certain que notre Numénius soit juif de naissance, du moins pencherais-je à en faire un sémite." Dodds, "Numenius and Ammonius," 6 f. is skeptical: "Incidentally, I have some difficulty in accepting the tentative suggestion of Bigg and Puech that Numenius himself was a Jew."

[127] H. Leon, *The Jews of Ancient Rome* (1960), p. 103, and nos. 142, 143, and 305 in the Appendix of Inscriptions.

[128] So Dodds, "Numenius and Ammonius," p. 6.

have been a Jew on grounds of orthodoxy alone. There must have been many nominal Jews, especially in the Hellenistic cities, whose loyalty to Jewish traditions was limited to parentage or, in the case of educated persons, to a desire to preserve certain aspects of their tradition, albeit in hellenized form.[129] On the other hand, it is certainly correct to suggest, as does Dodds, that Numenius' knowledge of and sympathy for Judaism can be understood equally well by recalling that his city of origin was Apamea in Syria where Jews were resident.[130] As in the case of "Longinus" we must be content with the recognition that conclusive evidence is lacking on either side and that the question as it stands is unanswerable.

Porphyry

In our brief study of Numenius we ascertained two important elements in emergent Neoplatonism: first, that there was a conscious effort from the very beginning to incorporate the wisdom of non-Greeks into its philosophical system, and second, that this interest led to a considerable knowledge and appreciation of Moses as a worthy representative of ancient oriental wisdom. It is unfortunate that Plotinus, the link between Numenius and Porphyry and the true father of Neoplatonism, left no writing which mentions either Moses or the Jews. His successor, biographer, and secretary, Porphyry, however, does mention them on several occasions.[131] In fact Porphyry may be considered as typical of Neoplatonic attention to Eastern peoples and their wisdom.

One of his early writings, *De Philosophia ex Oraculis Haurienda*,[132] is an attempt to construct a philosophical-religious system on the basis of popular Greek and Eastern religious traditions. At one point

[129] Specific examples of such ex-Jews or acculturated Jews are discussed by Schürer, 3:135 ff.; see also below, pp. 76 ff.

[130] We know next to nothing about the Jewish population in Apamea. Josephus, *BJ* 2.479 mentions that the citizens spared the local Jews during the events in and around 70 c.e. For other references and a brief discussion, see Tcherikover, *Hellenistic Civilization*, p. 289, n. 71.

[131] On the life and writings of Porphyry, see J. Bidez, *Vie de Porphyre, le philosophe néo-platonicien* (1913; repr. 1964)), and R. Beutler, "Porphyrios," RE 43 (1953): 275-313. Porphyry was born in Tyre and referred to Phoenician as his native tongue (*Plot.* 17).

[132] Ed. G. Wolf (1856; repr. 1962).

he quotes an oracle of Apollo to the effect that the Hebrews, along with the Phoenicians, the Assyrians, and the Lydians had learned the many paths to heaven, i.e., possessed superior knowledge of the gods.[133] A second oracle announces that "only the Chaldeans and the Hebrews reached true wisdom, they who worship piously the self-born god." [134] Again, when questioned about the superiority of speech, reason, or law the oracle is reported by Porphyry to have replied in verse,

God the creator and king before all things, before whom the heaven, the earth, the seas and the hidden depths of hell tremble and whom the gods themselves hold in great awe; their law is the father, whom the pious Hebrews worship fervently.[135]

Thus in his early career at Tyre, in the Semitic East, Porphyry's writing indicates a high esteem for the god of the Hebrews.

From Tyre, Porphyry moved to Athens, where he studied under the famed literary critic, Longinus.[136] Here he left behind some of his earlier enthusiasm for the East and acquired the refined tools of literary criticism which he later employed in his attack on Christianity, *Adversus Christianos*.[137] In the course of this attack he had occasion to express his thoughts about the books of Moses as they were used and interpreted by Christians:

Some people who desire to find a solution to the low quality (*mochthēria*) of the Jewish scriptures rather than abandoning them, have resorted to explanations which are inconsistent and incongruous with what is written, thereby supplying approval and praise for themselves but no defense of the foreign things [i.e., the original words]. For they consider the plain words of Moses to be enigmas and they regard them as oracles full of hidden mean-

[133] Wolf, p. 140 = Eusebius, *Praep. Evang.* 9.10.2 (413a).
[134] Wolf, p. 141 = *Praep. Evang.* 9.10.4 (413c).
[135] Wolf, p. 142 = Augustine, *De civ. D.* 19.23, and Lactantius, *De ira Dei* 23.12.
[136] On his period of study with Longinus, see Beutler, "Porphyrios," pp. 276 f., and Bidez, *Vie*, pp. 29-36; this Longinus is not to be confused with the author of the treatise *On the Sublime* (above, pp. 56 ff.).
[137] The fragments of this treatise have been collected and edited by A. Harnack, *Porphyrius, "Gegen die Christen," 15 Bücher, Zeugnisse, Fragmente und Referate* (1916); cf. also A. B. Hulen, *Porphyry's Work Against the Christians* (1933), and E. R. Dodds, *Pagan and Christian in an Age of Anxiety* (1965), pp. 125-27.

70

ings; having duped their critical faculty by nonsense, they carry out their exegesis. . . .[138]

Like Celsus (see below, pp. 92 ff.)¯, he refuses to admit that the writings of Moses contain any hidden wisdom which can be brought to light by allegorical exegesis. Like Celsus, he notes that exegetes are driven to the use of allegory in order to overcome the baseness of the Jewish scriptures when taken at face value. In fact, however, this statement cannot be admitted as sound evidence concerning Porphyry's assessment of Moses. His rejection of allegory is directed against Christian exegetes, and Origen in particular, rather than against Jews.[139] As in the case of Celsus it is a strictly polemical argument designed to undermine the support for Christian doctrines which Christian exegetes derived from Jewish scriptures by means of allegorical and typological exegesis. Thus Porphyry used his skill as a literary critic not so much against the Jewish scriptures themselves as against Christian use of them.[140] This view gains support from a second fragment where Porphyry expresses himself on the question of the authorship of the Mosaic writings:

Again the following saying seems to be full of foolishness: "If you believed in Moses, you would believe in me, for he wrote concerning me" [John 5:46]. The fact is that nothing of Moses has survived, for all his writings are said to have been burned along with the temple. Everything written thereafter in the name of Moses was actually written 1180 years later by Ezra and his colleagues.[141]

[138] *Adv. Christ.* Fr. 39 = Eusebius, *Hist. Eccl.* 6.19.4.
[139] So Eusebius, *Hist. Eccl.* 6.19.4.
[140] Other examples of Porphyry's skill as a literary critic are Fr. 12, 15, 16 in which he points out contradictions between the different gospel writers; Fr. 9-10 where he indicates incorrect references by New Testament writers to the Jewish scriptures; and Fr. 30-33 where he points to inconsistencies in Paul's letters. Even more impressive are his conclusions concerning the dating of the book of Daniel (preserved by Jerome, *Comm. in Dan.*, Prol.) : "Porphyry wrote his twelfth book against the prophecy of Daniel, denying that it was composed by the person to whom it is ascribed in its title, but rather by some individual living in Judaea at the time of the Antiochus who was surnamed Epiphanes. He furthermore alleged that "Daniel' did not foretell the future so much as he related the past, and lastly that whatever he spoke of up till the time of Antiochus contained authentic history, whereas anything he may have conjectured beyond that point was false, inasmuch as he could not have foretold the future." The translation is from *Jerome's Commentary on Daniel,* tr. G. L. Archer (1958) , p. 15.
[141] *Adv. Christ.* Fr. 68 = Macarius Magnes, *Apocriticus* 3.3. Porphyry obviously

71

The purpose of the statement is again purely polemical in that it seeks to deprive Christianity of any claim to antiquity on the basis of the Mosaic writings. So much does Porphyry's conclusion contradict the common presuppositions of Jews, pagans, and Christians concerning the Mosaic authorship of the Pentateuch that he himself does not insist on its acceptance, and in the *De Abstinentia,* written after the *Adversus Christianos,* the idea is entirely forgotten. In the present polemical writing his chief goal is to demonstrate that Christians may not use the Jewish scriptures to claim that their Messiah was prophesied in writings of such great antiquity.[142]

Porphyry's continuing sympathy for Judaism is reflected again by his use of Moses in his treatise *De Abstinentia ab Esu Animalium,*[143] a defense of vegetarianism written to a certain Castricius who had renounced the practice of abstinence from meat. In book 4, Porphyry argues against Castricius that certain wise men and nations had abstained from meat and thus offer solid precedents for the continuing practice of abstinence. After discussing meat abstinence among the early Greeks and the priests of Egypt, he introduces the example of the Jews whom he describes as "well-known to us." He mentions the three parties of the Jews—Pharisees, Sadducees, Essenes—and then simply copies Josephus' extensive account of the Essenes (*BJ* 2.120-160). In 4.14 he adds an excerpt (with minor variations) from Josephus (*Ap.* 2.213) to the effect that Moses forbade the killing of

---

possessed direct or indirect knowledge of the passage in 4 Ezra 14:21 ff. where Ezra laments the loss of law books by fire and beseeches God to allow him to rewrite everything from the beginning. Harnack and others have argued that the pagan arguments in the *Apocriticus* of Magnes Macarius (*ca.* 400 C.E.) derive indirectly from Porphyry. Harnack described the process of transmission as follows: Porphyry wrote his *Adversus Christianos ca.* 270; an anonymous two-book excerpt of it was made *ca.* 300; Macarius then used this two-volume excerpt to represent the position of the pagan in his *Apocriticus.* For Harnack's arguments, see *Porphyrius,* pp. 7-10, 27, and his *Kritik des Neuen Testaments von einem griechischen Philosophen des 3. Jahrhunderts* (1911), pp. 96-144; cf. also Hulen, *Porphyry's Work,* pp. 8 f.

[142] Although we lack the details of Porphyry's arguments against this type of Christian exegesis, the main thrust is evident in the brief sentence in Fr. 68: "It cannot be shown that Christ is anywhere called God, or that God is called word or demiurge. And who ever said that Christ is (to be) crucified?" These are standard Jewish arguments, repeated later by Julian; cf. Hulen, *Porphyry's Work,* pp. 32 f., and J. Vogt, *Kaiser Julian und das Judentum* (1939), pp. 16 f.

[143] On the background of the writing, see Beutler, "Porphyrios," pp. 291 f., and Bidez, *Vie,* pp. 98-102.

young birds and of animals used for labor even though they may belong to enemies.[144] To this Porphyry appends his own comment:

And he [Moses] was not afraid that these animals who were thus spared would multiply and cause a famine among humans, for he knew that prolific animals are short-lived and that they disappear rapidly when they are denied human care, and that beyond this there are other types of animals which attack those that multiply (pp. 251.14–252.1, ed. Nauck).

There can be little doubt that this concluding explanation represents Porphyry's own view, because it is nowhere else attributed to Moses, and because Castricius had used the exact counterargument, i.e., animals must be killed in order to prevent them from consuming the human food supply, to support his renunciation of abstinence. It should also be noted that Porphyry has overlooked or forgotten his earlier argument that none of Moses' writings survived the burning of the temple. He affirms, or at least he finds it convenient to accept Josephus' affirmation, that Moses is the author of the Jewish laws.

Although Porphyry seldom mentions Moses, his attitude is clearly one of respect. His esteem for the Jews as a people continued throughout his life, although the exuberance of his early years as reflected in *De Philosophia* seems to have diminished somewhat subsequent to his association with Longinus and Plotinus.[145] In knowledge of the biblical writings and in his critical analysis of them he knew no equal among pagan writers. Had we the good fortune to possess the full fifteen books of his *Contra Christianos* we would undoubtedly know much more of his attitude toward Moses. Given our present information we can only surmise that he treated him, as in *Abst.* 4.14, as an authoritative representative of ancient oriental wisdom.

Pseudo-Galen

Under the category of Porphyry's references to Moses, most critics have included a passage from a writing which bears the title *Galēnou*

---

[144] P. 251.9-14, ed. Nauck. In his citation of the *Contra Apionem,* Porphyry makes two changes which reveal his special interests. To Moses' prohibition against killing animals that seek refuge in houses, he adds that if he may not kill them "how much less may we eat them," and in the following sentence he has changed Josephus' simple *ergazesthai* to the compound *synergazesthai,* thereby emphasizing the cooperative relationship between men and animals.

[145] So Vogt, *Kaiser Julian,* p. 16.

pros Gauron peri tou pōs empsychoutai ta embrya (*Ad Gaurum*).[146]
The argument of the treatise is that the soul does not enter the embryo
until the moment of birth and that it is not a living being until this
moment. The bulk of the writing is given to a defense of this thesis,
which the author claims to have derived directly from Plato (2.1). He
argues against those who propose different interpretations of Plato
and advances a number of Platonic texts in support of his own position
(3.1–9.5). In 10.1 he announces that he can prove his point—that
the embryo possesses no life prior to the moment of birth—even
apart from Plato. But after a brief discussion of the similarities between the development of the embryo and ship-building, he returns
to his more dogmatic stance in 10.6 where he reasserts his view that
the soul enters the body, without force, at the moment of birth. In
11.1 he resumes his method of argument from ancient authority and
cites the theatrical reenactments of the Promethean creation story:

> As I have witnessed in the theater, those who play Prometheus are forced
> to make the soul enter the body while it (*plasma*) is lying on the ground;
> the ancients probably did not intend the myth to represent the entrance
> of the soul as something forced but rather to show that the entrance of the
> soul took place after birth and when the body was formed.

Then in 11.1 he cites the creation of man according to Gen. 2:7
as a second authority:

> The theologian of the Hebrews too seems to signify this when he says that
> when the human body was formed and had received all of its bodily work-
> manship, God breathed the spirit upon it for a living soul.[147]

---

[146] Ed. K. Kalbfleisch (1895). As far as I have been able to determine, no independent work has been done on the *Ad Gaurum* since Kalbfleisch's first and only
edition. Among those who have accepted Kalbfleisch's attribution of the writing
to Porphyry are J. Vogt, *Kaiser Julian*, p. 17, and Hulen, *Porphyry's Work*, p. 27.
The only dissent from Kalbfleisch's position was raised by Beutler, "Porphyrios,"
RE 43 (1953) : 290: "Trotz des *consensus omnium* . . . gibt es Bedenken gegen die Zu-
wendung an P[orphyrios] . . . ." Unfortunately Beutler does not discuss the question further. He concludes that while the writing itself may not be Porphyry's, it
still contains "porphyrianisches Gedankengut."

[147] ὅ δὴ καὶ ὁ τῶν Ἑβραίων θεολόγος σημαίνειν ἔοικεν,
ὅταν πεπλασμένου τοῦ ἀνθρωπίνου σώματος (καὶ)
ἀπειληφότος πᾶσαν τὴν σωματικὴν δημιουργίαν
ἐμφυσῆσαι τὸν θεὸν αὐτῷ εἰς ψυχὴν ζῶσαν λέγῃ τὸ πνεῦμα.

Compare the translation in Festugière, *Révélation*, 3:285.14-18. Festugière's is the
only translation known to me, other than Hulen's somewhat inaccurate rendering
in *Porphyry's Work*, p. 27.

74

As in the case of Longinus, the reference to Gen. 2:7 is a paraphrase rather than a direct quotation.[148] Only *eis psychēn zōsan,* the crucial phrase for the author, is quoted directly. The author was not so much interested in an exact quotation as in adducing a further authority in support of his thesis that the soul enters the body only after the moment of birth.

The author of the Genesis passage, obviously Moses, is called *ho tōn Hebraiōn theologos.*[149] This is the only pagan writing in which Moses is called *theologos.* According to F. Kattenbusch's study of the term, its use here together with Prometheus would seem to conform to the older usage in which *theologos* was equivalent to *mythologos.* Thus Moses would fall under the rubric of ancient sages whose knowledge of the gods was expressed in mythological form; therefore, in order to bring to light their hidden meaning it is necessary to understand them as symbols and to interpret them allegorically.

As for the source of the quotation or paraphrase we cannot say whether the author knew only this one passage from Genesis, whether he inherited his information from an intermediary source, or whether his knowledge of Jewish scriptures was based on his own reading of the Greek text. We can only affirm that his respect for Moses was considerable inasmuch as he saw fit to cite him, on the same level with Promethean theater representations, as a witness for an important philosophical issue.

As noted above, the title of the MS attributes the writing to Galen.[150] F. Kalbfleisch, who is responsible for the only edition of the text, argues convincingly that it contradicts Galen's views at every point and cannot possibly be attributed to him. Against the attribution in the MS he argues that the writing comes from the pen of

---

[148] Gen. 2:7 (LXX): . . . καὶ ἐνεφύσησεν εἰς τὸ πρόσωπον αὐτοῦ πνοὴν ζωῆς, καὶ ἐγένετο ὁ ἄνθρωπος εἰς ψυχὴν ζῶσαν.

[149] On the use of *theologos,* see F. Kattenbusch, "Die Entstehung einer christlichen Theologie. Zur Geschichte der Ausdrücke θεολογία, θεολογεῖν, θεολόγος," ZTK 11 (1930) : 161-205. According to Kattenbusch the terms were used synonymously with *mythos* etc. by Plato and Aristotle. Only with the Stoics did the term lose some of its earlier connotations and take on the meaning of a normative and critical examination of matters relating to the deity. Philo uses *theologos* twice of Moses (*Mos.* 2.115, *Praem.* 53). Clement of Alexandria uses it once (*Strom.* 1.[22.]150.4).

[150] According to Kalbfleisch (pp. 3 f.) the MS was discovered bound together with two writings of Galen. Between 1840, when it was first discovered at Mount Athos by M. Minas, and 1895 when it was published by Kalbfleisch, it was naturally assumed that the writing belonged to Galen.

Porphyry: (1) the rich and colored style resembles Porphyry's; (2) certain key ideas, phrases, and terms appear in similar form in Porphyry and *Ad Gaurum*, e.g., offsprings are always inferior to their begetters; (3) the common Neoplatonic notion that to know one's soul is to know the omnipresent soul occurs in both; (4) Iamblichus informs us that according to Porphyry the embryo received its soul at the moment of birth; (5) the eleventh-century Byzantine scholar Michael Psellus records in his *De Omnifaria Doctrina* (115) that Porphyry wrote a treatise on this very subject, in which he maintained that the embryo possessed neither life nor soul.[151]

These arguments are interesting but not entirely convincing. The occasional verbal argeements could be explained as borrowings either by Porphyry from *Ad Gaurum* or vice versa, or by both from common Neoplatonic tradition. The main argument, that the two authors share significant ideas of Neoplatonism, is open to the same criticism. In the same vein, his argument that Porphyry wrote a book on the same topic as our writing proves only what it in fact states; it does not prove that Porphyry is the author of this particular writing. In other words Kalbfleisch's arguments prove only that the writing emanated from Neoplatonic circles. One additional factor is the reference to Moses in *Ad Gaurum* 11.1. In his only undisputed reference to Moses, Porphyry uses the term *nomothetēs*, which is by far the most common designation of Moses in pagan and Christian literature. *Ad Gaurum* calls him *theologos*. This bit of evidence is hardly decisive, but it should raise some further doubt about Kalbfleisch's conclusion on the question of authorship.

Conclusion

In our discussion of Moses as a philosophical lawgiver the question of sources has arisen repeatedly. For Numenius one source of information was his own knowledge of Jewish scriptures. Conversely, there is no direct evidence that Hecataeus of Abdera, Strabo, or Pompeius Trogus possessed a firsthand knowledge of the biblical writings.[152]

[151] Kalbfleisch, pp. 11 ff.

[152] According to Heinemann, "Moses," p. 361, and V. Tcherikover, "Jewish Apologetic Literature Reconsidered," *Eos* 48 (1956) : 177, among others, there is no evidence that Greeks read the Greek Bible prior to the advent of Christianity.

In fact our analysis has pointed in a quite different direction, namely, the influence of Jewish apologetics and the role of Moses as the national hero par excellence in this tradition.[153] In the middle of the second century B.C.E. the apologist Aristobulus, writing in Alexandria, claimed that Plato borrowed his legislation from Moses and that Homer and Hesiod appropriated the idea of a holy sabbath day from Jewish scriptures.[154] Sometime before 150 B.C.E. the apologist Eupolemus represented Moses as the first sage and claimed that he had taught the skill of writing to the Jews from whom the Phoenicians and finally the Greeks had learned to write.[155] In a similar vein, though more extravagant in its claims, is the so-called Moses romance of Artapanus (*ca.* 100 B.C.E.).[156] According to this tale Moses was the teacher of Orpheus; he invented cranes for lifting stones, and machines for drawing water and waging war; he discovered philosophy and created the basic elements of Egyptian religion, complete with its worship of animals; finally, for having interpreted (*hermeneia*) the sacred writings, he was honored by the Egyptian priests as a god and named Hermes.[157] In the first century of the Christian period, Philo described Moses as "the greatest and most perfect of men" and the ideal lawgiver, king, priest, and prophet,[158] while Josephus asserted that he was the most ancient of all lawgivers, and that the wisest Greek philosophers—Pythagoras, Anaxagoras, Plato, and the Stoics— were all dependent on him (*Ap.* 2.154,168).

From Judaism the theme of Moses' priority vis-à-vis the Greeks passed into Christian writings. Justin (*Apol.* 44), Tatian (*Ad Graec.*

---

[153] For general discussions of Moses in Jewish apologetic literature, see Is. Lévy, *La légende de Pythagore* (1927), pp. 137-53; K. Thraede, "Erfinder (II) ," RAC 5 (1962) : 1247 f.; D. Georgi, *Die Gegner des Paulus im 2. Korintherbrief* (1964) , pp. 148-82; and literature cited above, p. 16, n. 3.

[154] *Apud* Eusebius, *Praep. Evang.* 13.12.1 (664ab) ; 13.12.13-16 (667d-668c). On Aristobulus, see N. Walter, *Der Thoraausleger Aristobulus* (1964), with full bibliography and a discussion of previous research.

[155] *Apud* Clem. Alex., *Strom.* 1.[23.]153.4 = Eusebius, *Praep. Evang.* 9.26.1 (431c) . On Eupolemus, see Schürer 3:474-77, and Freudenthal, *Hellenistische Studien*, pp. 105-30.

[156] On Artapanus, see Schürer, 3:477-80, and Braun, *History and Romance*, pp. 26-31, 97-102.

[157] *Apud* Eusebius, *Praep. Evang.* 9.27.3-5 (432a-c) .

[158] *Mos.* 1.1, 2.2 f. As usual, Philo was more "reserved" than his predecessors and limits Greek borrowing from Moses to a few cases, e.g., Heraclitus (*Leg.All.*1. 108, *Quis. Her.* 214) .

40-41), Clement of Alexandria,[159] Origen,[160] and Eusebius[161] in turn repeat the traditional claims that Moses lived before the Greeks and that they derived much of their philosophy and mythology from him. In short, there grew up between the second century B.C.E. and the fourth century C.E. a considerable apologetic literature in which Moses was set against and above the heroes of Greek civilization.[162]

Is there any evidence that this apologetic material influenced pagan writers in the pre-Christian era? It has been argued, notably by V. Tcherikover, that pre-Christian Jewish apologetic literature was directed not at Greeks but at different segments of diaspora Judaism itself;[163] that the exaltation of Judaism in this literature arose initially among Hellenistic Jews who "found it easier to cling to Judaism as long as they knew that Judaism stood on an equal level with Hellenism"; that the praise of Judaism became "an everlasting source of consolation" in the face of aggressive anti-semitism; and that the polemic against paganism aimed not at the pagan world but at renegade Jews who renounced Judaism and severed their ties with the Jewish community (180 f.). As for apologetic literature proper, i.e., a defense of Judaism directed at non-Jews, Tcherikover claims that it appeared only under the Roman Empire and that its dissemination was never very broad (180).

Granting at least the partial wisdom of Tcherikover's thesis with respect to the intended audience of this literature, there remain nonetheless some unanswered questions.[164] Where did Hecataeus of Abdera,

---

[159] Clement devotes a lengthy section of the *Stromateis* to the question of Moses' great antiquity; *Strom.* 1.[21.]101-150.

[160] *C. Cels.* 4.21; cf. 1.18, 6.7, 6.43.

[161] Eusebius devotes nearly five of the fifteen books of the *Praeparatio* (9-13) to an elaborate defense of the thesis that Greek wisdom as a whole was derived from the Jewish scriptures.

[162] Cf. J. Pépin, "Le 'challenge' Moïse-Homère aux premiers siècles chrétiens," *Revue des Sciences Religieuses* 29 (1955) : 105-22.

[163] "Jewish Apologetic," pp. 169-93. Tcherikover denies not only the fact but even the possibility of such an influence. He argues that books were few in number and high in cost, that book sellers concentrated on established classics, and that the attitude of Greeks toward Jews in Egypt was generally hostile. Any one of these considerations would suffice, he says, to rule out the notion of a "widespread Jewish literary propaganda among Greeks" (171).

[164] Tcherikover himself admits that "single copies [of apologies] would of course be given by the author directly to Greeks . . ." (173). Beyond this I think it not unfair to suggest that he has overreacted in his desire to correct what he regards as a serious misunderstanding of pre-Christian Jewish apologetic literature.

Strabo, and Pompeius Trogus procure their information about Moses and the Jews? How does one explain the statements of Theophrastus, Megasthenes, Clearchus, and Hermippus (see above, p. 36, n. 30) to the effect that the Jews were a nation of philosophers? The answer must be that their sources, whether written or oral, were Jewish and that these sources must be characterized as patently apologetic. Regardless of their intended audience, they were formulated in direct reaction to the non-Jewish environment, and it is only natural to assume that they could be and were pressed into "foreign" duty under the proper circumstances. Hecataeus, Theophrastus, and Megasthenes, each of whom flourished around 300 B.C.E., reflect the earliest stage, quite probably oral, of this apologetic tradition. In subsequent centuries the form and details of the tradition changed in accordance with the specific demands of time and place, but one basic element remained constant: Moses, the lawgiver of the Jews, was in no way inferior and in many respects superior to his pagan counterparts. A second contributing factor to this tradition was the utopian character of Hellenistic ethnographic literature in general. In the case of Moses and the Jews, this tendency was further heightened by a persistent fascination among Greeks for eastern peoples—Jews, Babylonians, and Indians—in particular. Thus in areas and at times when relations between Jews and pagans did not suffer from political or religious inflammations, one image of Moses, as a wise lawgiver, remained essentially unchanged in pagan literature.

For our purposes, however, even the "single copy" would be sufficient to explain the material in Hecataeus and Strabo if we assume that they made inquiries in the Alexandrian Jewish community concerning the origins of the Jewish people.

2. Moses as a Deficient Lawgiver

Not all pagans were as sympathetically inclined to Moses and his laws as the authors we have discussed in the previous section. In the main these writers came from cities in the eastern portion of the Mediterranean basin: Hecataeus from Abdera but resident at Alexandria in its early years, Strabo from Amaseia in Pontus, Numenius from Apamea, and Porphyry from Tyre. In contrast to what we might call this Eastern, largely Greek, view of Moses stand two quite different traditions, one emanating from Alexandria and appearing also in Antioch, and the other associated with Rome in the post-Augustan era. In these three power centers of the Hellenistic and Roman imperial dynasties there emerged an entirely different view of Moses the lawgiver. We turn our attention first to Rome.

Quintilian

The first Latin author of the post-Augustan era to mention Moses is the rhetor Quintilian. About the year 92, at the end of his long career as a teacher and practitioner of rhetoric, he acceded to the demands of his friends that he set down in systematic form his views on rhetoric (*Institutio Oratoria*).[1] Book 3 of the *Institutio* focuses on the types, the aims, and the elements of rhetoric including speeches concerning praise and blame (3.7.1-28). As virtue can be praised, he says, so vice can be denounced in two basic ways, by directing our attention to the living or to the dead:

> Infamy comes to some after death, like Maelius, whose house was razed to the ground, or Marcus Manlius, whose first name was banned from the family for all time. And we hate the parents of evil offspring; and it is notorious for founders of cities to have brought together a people which is bent on the destruction of others, as for example the creator of the Jewish superstition. The laws of the Gracchi are despised, as is any base example handed down to posterity, such as the sexual practise which a Persian is said to have initiated on a woman of Samia (3.7.21).

The allusion to Moses is significant in several respects. The fact that the name itself is not mentioned can only mean that Moses was sufficiently well known in Roman literary circles so that the allusion alone was enough to alert the reader to the figure in question. A second point concerns the literary genre and purpose of the *Institutio*. Some regard the allusion to Moses as a personal outburst of Quintilian's anti-Jewish sentiment.[2] Others, notably F. H. Colson, have pointed out that Quintilian is here dealing with rhetorical *topoi*, stock subjects that rhetors might and probably did select as examples, and that to this extent he is not necessarily identifying himself with specific opinions.[3]

In fact we know precious little about Quintilian's view of Judaism. That he once defended Berenice, daughter of the Herodian Agrippa and mistress of the Emperor Titus, tells us nothing because he probably had little choice in the matter. His relationship to Flavius Clemens, his wife Flavia Domitilla, and their much disputed religious affiliation is equally ambiguous.[4] Quintilian (4.Prooem.2) tells us that

---

[1] In the preface to book 1, he says that he undertook the project after twenty years of teaching rhetoric. His birth, at Calgurris in Spain, is normally placed around 35 c.e.; the date of his death is unknown.

[2] E.g., Reinach, *Textes*, p. 285, n. 2; J.-A. Hild, "Les juifs à Rome devant l'opinion et dans la littérature," REJ 11 (1885) : 166 ff.

[3] Colson, "Quintilian, the Gospels and Christianity," CR 39 (1925) : 168, n. 4.

[4] For a discussion of the relevant issues, see Leon, *The Jews of Ancient Rome*, pp. 33-35, and W. H. C. Frend, *Martyrdom and Persecution in the Early Church* (1965) , pp. 214-17, and the literature there cited.

81

the Emperor Domitian, who was Flavius' cousin, had designated Quintilian as the tutor of Flavius' and Flavia's children. From Xiphilinus' epitome of Dio Cassius (67.14.1-2) we learn that in 95 Flavius and Flavia were convicted of atheism, as a result of which Flavius was executed and Flavia exiled of the island of Pandateria. Dio's words clearly indicate that the atheism in question was Judaism: "The charge against both was atheism, for which charge many others who had drifted into Jewish practises were condemned. . . ." Beclouding the issue is the fact that Eusebius (*Hist. Eccl.* 3.18.4) some two hundred years later makes Domitilla a Christian and identifies the island as Pontia, while wrongly making her Flavius' niece instead of his wife. One would probably be justified in disregarding Eusebius' testimony were it not that a Flavia Domitilla is known to have donated private land which was used for Christian burials in the second century.[5] But in either case, be she Jewish, Christian, or neither, it would be extremely difficult to specify how her religious affiliation could have affected Quintilian's feelings about Judaism and hence about Moses.

But even if we hesitate to identify Quintilian's personal feelings with the hostile tone of his words, they remain a significant witness to the more or less official attitude toward Moses in Roman literary circles of the late first century. Quintilian was obviously a leading figure of his time and his opinions must be regarded as reliable reflections of contemporary thought. The fact that essentially the same view of Moses appears in Tacitus and Juvenal is further evidence that a new image of Moses, prompted no doubt by the series of conflicts with the Jews under Tiberius, Caligula, Claudius, and finally Vespasian, had established itself in the post-Augustan era.

Tacitus

Not long after Quintilian's death Tacitus published his *Histories,* covering the period from 69 to the death of Domitian in 96. After the traditional fashion of Hellenistic and Roman historiography,

---

[5] Leon (35) reconciles the conflicting notices by the suggestion that Flavia may have converted to Christianity after her return from exile. As to the burial site itself, Frend notes that it probably was purchased for Flavia's freedmen, not for herself, and that contrary to earlier opinion the land was not used for Christian burials until the mid-second century (216 f.) .

Tacitus introduced an ethnographic excursus on the Jews in book five as a prelude to his narrative of the capture of Jerusalem in 70.[6] In form the excursus follows the standard ethnographic model: the early history of the people (5.2-3); their religious and social customs (5.4-5); the topography of the land (5.6-8); and events of more recent history (5.9-10). From the content and length of the excursus it would appear that he must have consulted a number of sources, although as was his general practice he nowhere mentions these sources by name. In 5.2, for instance, he lists five different theories concerning the origins of the Jews but gives no indication either of their respective proponents or of his own assessment of their validity. Again in 5.3, with no mention of his source or any specific revelation of his own position, he presents what he regards as the *communis opinio* on Jewish origins.[7] The account is a version of the Alexandrian tale of the expulsion of the Jews from Egypt and will be discussed below (pp. 127 f.) together with the Alexandrian authors.

In the following section (5.4-5) Tacitus turns his attention to the laws which Moses established in the new city of Jerusalem:

(4) In order to secure the loyalty of the people to him for all time, Moses introduced new practices which are opposed to those of all other men. They regard as profane everything which is sacred to us, and conversely they allow everything which we abhor. They set up in the sanctuary a statue of the animal by whose guidance they escaped their wandering and thirst, whereas they sacrifice a ram in apparent derision of Ammon; an ox is also sacrificed because the Egyptians worship Apis. They abstain from pork in recollection of the plague, because the scab which attacks this animal once infected them. Even today they recall their prolonged starvation of former days with frequent fasts. And the unleavened Jewish bread is retained as evidence of the grains which they stole. They say that they decided to rest on the seventh day because it brought an end to their troubles; later on,

[6] The *Histories*, of which we possess approximately five of the perhaps fourteen original books, contain two additional excurses: 2.3 on the temple of the Paphian Venus, and 4.83 f. on the origins of the Serapis cult. According to R. Syme, *Tacitus* 1 (1958): 311, ethnographic and geographic excurses disappear altogether in the later *Annals* where they are replaced by digressions on Roman antiquities.

[7] On the sources of 5.2-5, see H. Lewy, "Tacitus on the Origin and Manners of the Jews" [in Hebrew with English summary], *Zion* 8 (1943): 17-26; I. Levy, "Tacite et l'origine du peuple juif," *Latomus* 5 (1946): 331-40; and A. M. A. Hospers-Jansen, *Tacitus over de Joden* (1949), pp. 110-19 (English summary of same, 190-95). For kind assistance in the translation of the article of H. Lewy I am indebted to Prof. Sheldon Isenberg.

attracted by laziness, they also made the seventh year a time of no work. . . . (5) These practices, whatever their origin, are supported by their antiquity; the other institutions are foul and perverse and have survived only by their depravity.

Although Moses figures as something of a hero in the desert, the picture changes drastically with his arrival in Jerusalem. Here he becomes the prototype, historically and symbolically, of Jewish xenophobia and misanthropy. In form as well as content Tacitus follows the same method as Hecataeus, Pompeius Trogus, and others in explaining the origins of the Mosaic legislation in terms of reactions to specific events of the exodus: the ass is honored because it led them to water in the desert (see below, p. 125, n. 28); they abstain from pork because pigs suffer from the same disease as a result of which the Jews were expelled from Egypt;[8] their frequent fasts and unleavened bread commemorate their hasty departure from Egypt; they celebrate the seventh day because their wandering ceased after six days in the desert; and they sacrifice the ram and the ox because these animals are sacred to the Egyptians.[9] The only new element is his mention of the sabbath year, which he attributes to the love for inactivity, not of Moses, but of the Jews.[10]

Some of this information appears to indicate a firsthand knowledge of the Jewish community, e.g., the mention of the reason behind the unleavened bread and the term *ferunt* ("they say") in his explanation of the sabbath. In the main, however, the material of 5.4 reflects widespread beliefs about Jewish customs. The tone is set in the introductory statement: "They hold everything profane which is sacred to us, and they allow everything forbidden by us." Here, too, Tacitus shows his dependence on traditional evaluations of the Mosaic laws. Hecataeus of Abdera, in an otherwise friendly statement, describes the customs introduced by Moses as "unsocial and hostile to foreigners" (see above, p. 35); in Diodorus Siculus 34.1.3 Moses is presented as the one who instituted the "misanthropic and strange customs of

---

[8] Cf. Plutarch, *Quaest. Conv.* 4.5.3.

[9] Cf. the almost identical statement attributed to Manetho, *apud* Josephus, *Ap.* 1.239: "He [Osarsiph = Moses] ordained that they should . . . not abstain from the flesh of any of the animals held in special reverence in Egypt, but should kill and consume them all . . . ."

[10] See the discussion in Schürer, 1:35-37.

the Jews" (see below, p. 125); and Apollonius Molon, Lysimachus, and others claimed, according to Josephus (*Ap*. 2.145), that the Jews learned vice rather than virtue from the laws of Moses.

At two critical points, however, Tacitus seems to assert his independence vis-à-vis the traditional negative view of Moses. In the opening sentence of 5.4 he moves beyond the simple description of Moses' legislative activity by assigning a motive for it: *"in order* to secure the loyalty of the people to himself for all time Moses introduced new practices. . . ."* For this there is no exact parallel in earlier writers. Strabo ascribes a theological motive for Moses' departure from Egypt, but none for his legislation as such. On Tacitus' part the ascription of a motive falls in line with his image of Moses as a forceful leader of his people and as the symbolic representative of the Jews. Yet another modification of the traditional picture appears in the remark which serves as the transition from 5.4 to 5.5:

> These practices, whatever their origin, are supported by their antiquity; the other institutions are foul and perverse and have survived only by their depravity.[11]

The remark introduces two new factors. First, the phrase "whatever their origin" strengthens the general impression that Tacitus is reporting common opinion rather than his own position, at least with respect to the genesis of the practices described in 5.4. Second, it distinguishes Moses and his customs, which have at least long tradition in their favor, from later, post-Mosaic institutions about which no good can be spoken. This distinction is reminiscent of Strabo who likewise separates Moses and his early successors from later superstitious and tyrannical leaders whose innovations were unworthy of Moses (see above, p. 43). For Tacitus' view of Moses, this brief comment in 5.5 is of real significance. Taken with the emergence of Moses as the hero of the exile (5.3), it means that he regards him with something akin to grudging respect. In one breath he holds him responsible for the aberrant religious practices of the Jews, while in the next he seems to regard the principle behind his legislation as

---

[11] The "other" customs are enumerated in 5.5 and include the practice whereby proselytes contributed two drachmas annually to the temple in Jerusalem, the xenophobia and separatism of the Jews, and their refusal to set up statues of the emperor.

85

a wise political stratagem, attributes the worst of Jewish practices to later times, and concedes at least the antiquity of the Mosaic laws. Thus while his view of Moses lacks the idealizing tendencies of Hecataeus or Strabo, it should not be confused with Lysimachus' or Apion's where redeeming features are altogether lacking.

Juvenal

Like Tacitus in some of its details is the passing mention of Moses by Juvenal. In his fourteenth satire, published around 125 c.e., Juvenal lays bare the manifold bad habits which are compounded as they pass from parents to children.[12] As one example he cites the father who observed the Jewish sabbath and abstained from pork, but whose sons became Jewish proselytes:[13]

Having grown accustomed to disdain Roman customs, they learn and honor and revere the Jewish law and everything that Moses handed down in his secret book, such as refusing to show the way to any but those who worship the same rites and leading only the circumcized to a desired fountain.[14]

The two examples cited from Moses' book, i.e., not to show the way to non-Jews and not to point out a fountain to the uncircumcised, are typical expressions of the charge of Jewish misanthropy.[15] According to Lysimachus, for example, Moses advised the Jews "to show goodwill to no man, to offer not the best but the worst advice" (see below, pp. 118 ff.), while Tacitus charged that among themselves Jews always show compassion "but with others they show hateful

---

[12] On the date of publication, and generally on Juvenal, see G. Highet, *Juvenal the Satirist* (1954), pp. 14-16, and the extensive literature cited throughout.

[13] On the apparently strong attraction of Judaism for certain aristocratic circles during the early reign of Augustus, see Leon, *The Jews of Ancient Rome*, pp. 11-14.

[14] 14.100-104; on the passage, see J. Bernays, "Die Gottesfürchtigen bei Juvenal," *Gesammelte Abhandlungen von Jacob Bernays*, ed. H. Usener (1885), 2:71-80; J. E. B. Mayor, *Thirteen Satires of Juvenal* (1888), 2:302-12; and Highet, *Juvenal*, p. 283, n. 3.

[15] H. J. Rose, "Juvenal xiv.103-4," CR 45 (1931): 127 cites Ps. 146:9 (LXX): "The Lord protects the proselytes . . . and destroys the road of the sinners" as explaining xiv.103, and Prov. 5:16-17 (LXX): "Do not let the water from your spring overflow . . . . Let it be for you only, and let no foreigner share it with you" as explaining xiv.104. This is hardly possible, for it demands a knowledge which no pagan, let alone Juvenal, possessed.

enmity" (*Hist.* 5.5). Juvenal undoubtedly knew Tacitus' works and may well have been inspired by his section on Moses.[16]

One peculiar note is Juvenal's remark that Moses wrote his laws in a secret book (*volumen arcanum*). Nowhere except in the later magical papyri are books of Moses called secret. One possible explanation is the tale in Diodorus Siculus according to which Antiochus Epiphanes discovered in the temple at Jerusalem the statue of a bearded man, obviously Moses, seated on an ass and holding a book (see below, p. 126). This story, together with the general knowledge that access to the temple was forbidden to outsiders, may have led Juvenal to the mistaken conclusion that the books of Moses were also forbidden to non-Jews. Be that as it may, Juvenal's three lines provide no new "information" about Moses. His own knowledge of Judaism, e.g., the sabbath, proselytes, abstention from pork, and circumcision, is typical of "informed" literary opinion. Similarly, his image of Moses as the author of practices which are contrary to Roman customs is drawn according to the accepted models of his time. For this reason the lines reveal rather less about Juvenal's personal reaction to Moses than about his real distaste for successful Jewish proselytism among Roman citizens.

Galen

The attitude toward Moses of the physician-philosopher Galen (129-*ca*.199) has received careful and extensive treatment by R. Walzer.[17] In his discussion he has taken care to set the passages within the context of Galen's own writings, while at the same time comparing his attitude toward Moses with that of other writers from Hecataeus to Porphyry. Thus I find myself in the happy situation of being able to rely almost entirely on the work of a predecessor, and the following discussion will be little more than a summary of that part of Walzer's work which concerns the figure of Moses.

---

[16] For a discussion of the possible contacts between Juvenal and Tacitus, see Highet, *Juvenal*, pp. 11 f.; 236, n. 13; 273, n. 7.

[17] *Galen on Jews and Christians* (1949); the work includes an introduction to Galen's thought, a critical text (Greek and Arabic), translations and lengthy discussions of each text.

Moses' Reliance on Faith Rather than Reason

Walzer notes the difference for Galen between relying on certain human authorities, like Hippocrates in medical affairs, and relying on divine authority. The former has a definite, albeit restricted, place in Galen's system, whereas the latter has little or no place at all:

They compare those who practise medicine without scientific knowledge to Moses, who framed laws for the tribe of the Jews, since it is his method in his books to write without offering proofs, saying "God commanded, God spoke."[18]

In this criticism of Moses from the standpoint of scientific logic and demonstration, Walzer suggests that Galen must have known, and rejected, the traditional Greek image of Moses as a divinely inspired lawgiver. The "God commanded, God spoke" recalls the similar statements of Hecataeus in Diodorus Siculus (see above, pp. 30 f.), where the authority of Moses' laws is made to depend on the deity who revealed them. Closer to Galen's own time is Strabo (see above, pp. 41 f.), where Moses is again presented as one of many lawgivers who claimed divine authority for their laws. Whether Galen possessed direct knowledge of Diodorus or Strabo is uncertain. What is certain is that knowing this traditional Greek Moses, Galen criticized him from a philosophical perspective which differed considerably from that of earlier writers who mentioned Moses and the Jews. Thus there begins in Galen's time a new phase in the development of pagan attitudes toward Moses. Galen, Celsus, and Julian continued to recognize Moses as a philosopher, much as Hecataeus and Strabo before them, but as one who needed to be criticized for serious philosophical deficiencies.

The three passages from Galen cited below use Moses' followers in much the same manner as the above passage uses Moses himself:

One might more easily teach novelties to the followers of Moses and Christ than to the physicians and philosophers who cling fast to their schools.[19]

[18] Walzer, pp. 10 f., discussed in pp. 18-23; the passage, preserved only in Arabic, is from Galen's work *On Hippocrates' Anatomy*.

[19] *De puls.* 3.3 (vol. 8, p. 657.1, ed. Kuehn). In this writing Galen attacks the physician Archigenes for relying on tradition rather than experiment and observation in his medical affairs.

. . . in order that one should not at the very beginning, as if one had come into the school of Moses and Christ, hear talk of undemonstrated laws, and that where it is least appropriate.[20]

If I had in mind people who taught their pupils in the same way as the followers of Moses and Christ teach theirs—for they order them to accept everything on faith—I should not have given you a definition.[21]

Here the followers of Moses and Christ are likened to schools of medicine or philosophy that rely on undemonstrated hypotheses. The crux of Galen's criticism is that the Jewish and Christian understanding of *pistis* was by and large foreign to Greek thinkers and could never suffice, at least as they understood the term, as an authority in philosophical or scientific matters. Thus Moses' chief source of authority (i.e., divine commands) becomes the main point of contention between Galen and the successors of Moses. The point at issue is summarized nicely by E. R. Dodds:

Had any cultivated pagan of the second century been asked to put in a few words the difference between his own view of life and the Christian one, he might reply that it was the difference between *logismos* and *pistis*, between reasoned conviction and blind faith. To any one brought up on classical Greek philosophy, *pistis* meant the lowest grade of cognition: it was the state of mind of the uneducated. . . .[22]

While Dodds's words are formulated primarily with Christians in mind, their relevance for Galen's view of Moses is readily apparent.

That Galen regards Moses as a philosopher is evident also in the following passage where he disputes with him on philosophical grounds:

Did our demiurge simply enjoin this [eyebrow] hair to preserve its length always equal, and does it strictly observe this order either from fear of its master's command, or from reverence for the god who gave this order, or is it because it itself believes it better to do this? Is not this Moses' way of treating nature, and is it not superior to that of Epicurus? The best way, of course, is to follow neither of these but to maintain like Moses the principle of

[20] *De puls.* 2.4 (vol. 8, p. 579.15, ed. Kuehn).
[91] Cf. Walzer, pp. 14 f. The quotation is preserved only in Arabic and occurred in a lost work entitled *Eis to prōton kinoun akinēton.* See also Walzer's discussion of the three passages, pp. 37-48.
[22] *Pagan and Christian in an Age of Anxiety* (1965), pp. 120 f.; cf. also the discussion in Walzer, pp. 48-56.

the demiurge as the origin of every created thing, while adding the material principle to it. For our demiurge created it to preserve a constant length, because this was better. . . . When he had determined to make it so, he set under part of it a hard body as a kind of cartilage, and under another part a hard skin attached to the cartilage through the eyebrows. For it was certainly not sufficient merely to will their becoming such: it would not have been possible for him to make a man out of a stone in an instant, by simply wishing so. It is precisely this point in which our own opinion and that of Plato and of the other Greeks who follow the right method in natural science differ from the position taken up by Moses. For the latter it seems enough to say that God simply willed the arrangement of matter and it was presently arranged in due order; for he believes everything to be possible with God, even should He wish to make a bull or a horse out of ashes. We however do not hold this; we say that certain things are impossible by nature and that God does not even attempt such things at all but that he chooses the best out of the possibilities of becoming.[23]

At issue is whether the demiurge can create anything whatsoever or whether he is limited by the givenness of matter and by his nature as a divine being. On this issue, Moses, here understood as a philosopher of creation, assumes a position between Epicurus, to whom he is superior, and Plato, to whom he is clearly inferior. Galen attributes to Moses the idea of a deity capable of unlimited creation, whereas Galen's demiurge is limited by the material cause. Certain things, he says, are impossible by nature. Thus the demiurge cannot make animals out of ashes or cause eyelashes—which is the example cited by Galen—to stand erect on a base of soft skin.

Once again Galen appears to be familiar with Greek traditions about Moses. His picture of Moses' demiurge recalls the passage about the Jewish deity in "Longinus." But as in the case of his criticism of Moses as lawgiver—where he effectively reversed the traditional Greek appreciation of Moses—Galen exercises his independent judgment by rejecting, at least implicitly, "Longinus' " appreciation of Moses' conception of the deity as an omnipotent creator. Of Galen's attitude to Moses and the Jews, Walzer (p. 2) says:

His judgments are unbiased and reveal a degree of understanding by no means common among the educated classes of his day. The subject is of

[23] *De usu partium* (vol. 3, p. 904, ed. Kuehn) ; cf. Walzer, pp. 11-13 and 23-27.

90

no immediate concern to him: he would scarcely have embarked upon writing a special criticism of Jewish and Christian life, as did his contemporary Celsus. . . . His observations resemble rather the "asides" of an actor on the stage.

If we ask whence Galen derived his information or image of Moses and why he saw fit to mention him, our answer must be that educated Greeks and Romans of the late Hellenistic and Imperial periods knew more about the Jews, Moses, and especially the first chapters of Genesis than one is wont to recognize. Walzer makes the very plausible suggestion that Galen's references to Moses "reflect a discussion which had been going on for some time in the higher strata of Roman society . . ." (2 f.). Moses in particular was well known among Greek writers associated with Rome as a philosophical lawgiver whose conception of the deity merited positive consideration. Galen is but a further witness to Moses' renown, and it is surely no coincidence that the aspects of Moses which he criticizes are precisely those which earlier writers had emphasized.

Apart from these inner-pagan traditions about Moses, other channels of information should be kept in mind in the particular case of Galen. Walzer points out that Galen's commentaries on Hippocrates were heavily dependent on a Rufus of Samaria, a wealthy Jewish physician who moved from Palestine to Rome in Galen's time and composed a compendium of earlier commentaries on Hippocrates.[24] To be sure, we do not know how well Galen knew Rufus, but his very existence enables us to locate an additional channel through which information about Moses and the Jews may have reached Galen and others of his time.[25]

[24] Walzer, pp. 8 f.; F. Pfaff, "Rufus aus Samaria. Hippocrates—Commentator und Quelle Galens," *Hermes* 67 (1932): 356-59. The information about Rufus is derived from Galen's commentary on Hippocrates, extant only in Arabic. The pertinent passage reads as follows in Pfaff's translation: ". . . nach Rufus aus Ephesus (hat) ein anderer Mann dieses Namens—ich erzähle davon noch bei einer anderen Lesart—aus dem Volke der Juden in unseren Tagen gelebt."

[25] Nock, *Gnomon* 23 (1951): 50, further adds that Galen's friend Flavius Boethus became governor of Judaea at about the time (*ca.* 162-166 c.e.) that Galen composed his *On Hippocrates' Anatomy*, in which the first reference to Moses occurs. In the course of their correspondence, the subject of the Jews was undoubtedly discussed.

Celsus

Sometime in the late second century C.E. the philosopher Celsus wrote the first known literary attack against Christianity.[26] The *Alēthēs Logos,* as Celsus himself called the work, represents the first attempt by a pagan to deliver a detailed refutation of this new religious phenomenon on legal, historical, and theological grounds.[27]

The figure of Moses, whom Celsus regards as the lawgiver of the Jews and the author of the Pentateuch, looms rather large in Celsus' work. The reason for this prominence is twofold: first, because Celsus devotes almost two books (1.28–2.79) to a criticism of Christianity from the standpoint of a Jew in dialogue with Jesus,[28] and second, because Christianity of the second century, with the exception of Marcion and some gnostic groups, claimed the Old Testament

[26] On the date of Celsus, see H. Chadwick's translation, with introduction and notes, *Origen Contra Celsum* (1953, corr. repr. 1965), xxvi ff. Chadwick settles on the period 177-80 as the probable date of composition. Of Celsus himself we know nothing save what we learn from Origen, who says that Celsus has "been dead a long time" (Praef. 4). He also states that Celsus was an Epicurean, although he can only surmise this from his writings (1.8), Origen knew two Epicureans who went under the name of Celsus, one a contemporary of Nero, the other of Hadrian and later times (*ibid.*). The second Celsus is probably identical with the Celsus to whom Lucian dedicated his *Alexander the False Prophet (ca.* 180). Lucian says that this Celsus wrote a work against magicians (*Alex.* 21), and Origen wonders whether our Celsus might not be "the same as the man who wrote several books against magic," presumably referring to the Celsus mentioned by Lucian. The argument against accepting Origen's analysis has been summarized succinctly by Chadwick: "Origen's Celsus at no point shows any signs of holding any Epicurean views whatsoever" (xxv). He further suggests that Origen accused Celsus of being an Epicurean in order to discredit him. I have followed Chadwick's translation throughout.

[27] Although the original work has disappeared, significant portions of it are reproduced in Origen's reply to Celsus, *Contra Celsum,* which Origen composed around 248 (on this date, see Chadwick, *Contra Celsum* xiv ff.). From this reply R. Bader has made a substantial, though not complete, reconstruction of Celsus' text which will serve as the basis for our discussion—*Der* ΑΛΗΘΗΣ ΛΟΓΟΣ *des Kelsos* (1940) ; cf. the discussion in Chadwick, *Contra Celsum* xxii-xxiv. My references will follow Bader's enumeration of the fragments. When part of a quotation appears in brackets, the bracketed portions represent Origen's comments, while the remainder contains Celsus' words. In substantial agreement with Bader's reconstruction is C. Andresen, *Nomos und Logos: Die Polemik des Kelsos wider das Christentum* (1955). Andresen concentrates on Celsus' philosophical position, but includes a chapter on the problems of reconstructing the text (pp. 8-43).

[28] On the Jewish sources behind *c. Cels.* 1.29-2.79, see M. Lods, "Étude sur les sources juives de la polémique de Celse contre les chrétiens," RHPR 21 (1941) : 1-33.

as its own sacred book and based much of its theology on typological and allegorical interpretations of it.

Celsus' attitude toward the Jews as a people is ambivalent. On the one hand he accords them faint praise because "they maintain their ancestral customs and observe a worship which may be very peculiar, but is at least traditional" (5.25). This is in accordance with his fundamental belief that "it is impious to abandon the customs which have existed in each locality from the beginning." [29] On the other hand, the Jews are not entirely free from the charge of rebellion against ancestral customs.[30] The Jews, he says, were Egyptians by race but rebelled against Egyptian customs and introduced new ideas (3.5). His distinctive criticism, however, is that the Jews and especially their lawgiver-theologian Moses have borrowed, distorted, and misunderstood the established truths of ancient pagan wisdom.

Moses and Monotheism

In 1.23 f. Celsus turns his polemic against Moses as the originator of Jewish monotheism:

The goatherds and shepherds who followed Moses as their leader were deluded by clumsy deceits into thinking that there was only one God . . . without any rational cause these goatherds and shepherds abandoned the worship of many gods . . . (1.23).

The attack is carried out at several levels. The *theological* argument focuses on two aspects of Moses' monotheism: first, his success in convincing his people to believe "that there was only one god" and his abandonment of "the worship of many gods" (1.23), and, second, the refusal of the Jews to recognize that there is one god who is worshiped under many names (1.24b, 5.41). Unfortunately, Celsus does not further identify the many gods of 1.23. In 5.6, however, he expresses surprise "that although they [the Jews] worship the heaven and the angels in it, yet they reject its most sacred and powerful

[29] 5.25; cf. Andresen, *Logos und Nomos,* pp. 64 ff. This is also his main criticism of Christianity (2.1, 5.33) and of pagan converts to Judaism (5.41).
[30] In 4.33 f., he rejects attempts to establish Jewish antiquity on the basis of descent from the patriarchs, whom he calls the "first offspring (*spora*) of sorcerers and deceivers." This is an attempt by Celsus to invalidate the common argument for the antiquity of the Jews on the basis that the patriarchs lived long before the Trojan War; cf. Josephus, *Ap.* 1.69-218.

parts, the sun, moon, and the other stars. . . ." On the basis of this single indication it would seem that the many gods are related to the heavenly bodies, who in turn were probably identified with the gods of traditional Greek and Egyptian religion, and that astral worship was the particular form of Celsus' polytheism.[31]

The second aspect of the theological argument concerns the explicit claim of the Jews that their god alone is the supreme deity and the implicit corollary that the gods worshiped by pagans are either inferior or nonexistent. To this claim Celsus replies in 5.41 with the affirmation of one supreme god and states "that it makes no difference whether we call Zeus the Most High or Zēn or Adonai, or Sabaoth or Amoun. . . ." [32] This second aspect is in apparent contradiction to the first, for it entails a belief in one supreme god and appears to ignore all others. In fact, however, there were a number of methods available in Celsus' time designed specifically for the harmonious reconciliation of monotheism and polytheism. From his statements in 1.24 it is apparent that he followed the method of positing one supreme god who was worshiped under many names by different nations.[33] Thus the issue between Celsus and Moses is not monotheism as such, but rather the unwillingness of Moses to go along with this particular form of theological syncretism.

The *historical* argument in 1.23 criticizes the Jews and their leader Moses for having overthrown their ancestral, i.e., Egyptian, polytheistic religion. In 3.5 he berates them for "revolting against the Egyptian community and despising the religious customs of Egypt," and in 5.41 he states that the consquence of this rebellion is that "they do not know the great God." The main thrust of Celsus' opposition to Moses is thus based on an argument from tradition, i.e., the chief sin of Moses is not monotheism proper but rather his departure from his ancestral Egyptian religion. For Celsus this alone was enough to condemn Moses' theology as a worthless innovation.

The third level of the argument is mainly *ad hominem* in character in that it applies common terms of depreciation to Moses and the

---

[31] Cf. the discussion in Chadwick, *Contra Celsum* xiv-xix, and M. Nilsson, *Geschichte der griechischen Religion,* 2 (1961 ²) : 575.

[32] Cf. 1.24 where the same argument appears.

[33] Cf. the view of the Middle Platonic philosopher, Maximus of Tyre: "The gods are one nature, but many names; it is only from ignorance that we give god different names in accordance with the various benefits he confers on us" (39.5) .

Jews. The basis of this third level is the standard pagan version of the exodus of the Jews from Egypt under the leadership of Moses. In 1.23, 26 and 5.41 he names Moses as the leader of the rebellion against the Egyptians. 1.23 states that he duped the Jews into following him by clumsy tricks, and 5.41 adds that the Jews were led on and deceived by Moses' sorcery. 1.26 adds the further note that the Jews "worship angels and are addicted to sorcery (*goēteia*) of which Moses was their teacher." [34] For the most part, these are stock phrases from earlier traditions about Moses and the exodus. In *Ap.* 2.145, for instance, Josephus mentions Apollonius Molon, Lysimachus, and others who malign Moses *hōs goēta kai apateōna*.[35] In 1.23 and 5.41 Celsus seems to have invested the terms with a specific content beyond their broader usage. Origen himself provides the clue to this content. In 1.45 he reports an earlier conversation with some Jews in Egypt in which he asked them how they met the charge of the Egyptians who rejected Moses "as a sorcerer who seemed to have performed his great deeds by magic." Again in 3.5 he reports the following Egyptian criticism of Moses: "they do not deny entirely the powerful miracles done by Moses, but claim that they were done by sorcery and not by divine power." Judging from 1.23 and 26 Celsus knew and used similar charges that the miracles which Moses performed at the time of the exodus were the result of trickery and not of divine power.[36] The point of this criticism is that while such miracles do possess some efficacy, their influence is limited to uneducated people and men of depraved moral character. In short this third level of the argument, which is little more than an argument from social inferiority, is added as a kind of *coup de grâce* to the more substantial—from Celsus' perspective—historical and theological criticisms. At the same time it provides an interesting insight into Celsus' polemical method: he overlooks no opportunity to demean or ridicule his opponent.

[34] The term *goēs* is also applied to Jesus in 1.71, 2.32, and 2.49.

[35] *Goēs* and *goēteia* were commonly used in Greek literature as terms of depreciation. In the *Symp.* 203D, Plato portrays his fictitious son of Poverty as *deinos goēs kai pharmakeus kai sophistēs*. In Polybius 4.20.5, *goēteia* occurs with *apatē* in reference to Ephorus' theory that music had been introduced into society for the purpose of deception and delusion. Lucian, *Nigr.* 15 uses *goēteia* in much the same way as Plato, i.e., as a caricature of the non-philosophical life. Finally, in *c. Gal.* 100A, Julian the Emperor refers to Paul as one who surpassed all other *goētes kai apateōnes*.

[36] The same charge is brought against Jesus' miracles in 1.6.

Moses and the Ancient Sages

In 1.16a Celsus argues that the Jews are not to be reckoned among the wise nations of the past:

[Again, when he makes a list of] ancient and wise men who were of service to their contemporaries and to posterity by their writings, [he rejects Moses from the list . . .] Linus, Musaeus, Orpheus, Pherecydes, Zoroaster the Persian and Pythagoras understood these doctrines, and their opinions were put down in books and are preserved to this day (1.16b).

The ground of Celsus' refusal to include the Jews is clearly that by virtue of their strange customs they do not share in the "ancient doctrine (*archaios logos*) which has existed from the beginning, which has always been maintained by the wisest nations and cities and wise men" (1.14). Thus, because Moses first incited the Jews to reject the ancient customs of Egypt (3.5), Celsus refuses to recognize him as one of the wise and ancient lawgivers. On this account Celsus diverges from certain of the earlier pagan writers on the Jews. Hecataeus of Abdera, Strabo, and Diodorus Siculus definitely included Moses among the ancient sages. The fact that the names of Musaeus and Orpheus appear in the list of both Celsus (1.16b) and Strabo (above, p. 45) arouses the suspicion that Celsus did not merely fail to include Moses but rather consciously removed his name from a list such as that of Strabo.

One passage in particular seems to show that Celsus was familiar with the admiration of Moses in certain pagan circles:

Moses heard of this doctrine which was current among the wise nations and distinguished men and acquired a name for divine power (*onoma daimonion*). . . . [But if, as you say,] he accepted wise and true doctrines and educated his own people by them, [what did he do deserving of criticism?] (1.21ab).[87]

If *daimonion* refers to magical abilities, Celsus may have known the traditions reflected in Pliny, Apuleius, and the magical papyri (see below, ch. 4). If, on the other hand, it refers to Moses' theological wisdom, Celsus may have in mind Strabo, Diodorus Siculus, "Longinus," or others like them.

[87] See the discussion of the fragment in Andreson, *Logos und Nomos*, pp. 11 f.

The precise content of the teaching which Moses supposedly borrowed from the ancients is not specified, although it is presumably related to the *archaios logos* of 1.14. Just prior to 1.21, Origen discusses the age of the cosmos (1.18 f), but in 1.21 proper the discussion focuses on various doctrines of god. Perhaps it is closer to Celsus' intention to see 1.21 as a general counterstatement to the claims of Jewish and Christian apologists who insisted that the Greeks had derived their wisdom from Moses.[38] In either case, however, the recognition that Moses acquired a name for divine power is tempered by the accusation that the doctrine was not Moses' own creation. Thus Celsus' criticism concerns not merely the content of Moses' thought but also the fact that he borrowed it from others and in so doing misunderstood and distorted it.

Certain other passages from Celsus reflect the criticism that Moses borrowed and either distorted or misunderstood ancient Greek mythology:

[He thinks, however, that] Moses [who] wrote about the tower [and the confusion of languages] corrupted the story about the sons of Aloeus when he composed the narrative about the tower (4.21a).

[Celsus also compares with] the story of Phaethon the narrative told [by Moses in Genesis] about Sodom and Gomorrah, that they were destroyed by fire on account of their sins (4.21b).

[But perhaps] Moses wrote these stories [about Adam in paradise] because he understood nothing, but did much the same as the poets of the Old Comedy, who mockingly wrote "Proetus married Bellerophon, and Pegasus came from Arcadia" (6.49b).

Again the quotations speak largely for themselves.[39] The tower of Babel (Gen. 11:1-9) is a corrupted version of the attempt by Aloeus'

---

[38] So Josephus, *Ap.* 2.257 ff.; Tatian, *Ad Graecos*, 40; and esp. Justin, *Apol.* 44 and 59 f.

[39] A further example of the historical argument is the charge that the account of Noah's flood is "a debased and unscrupulous version of the story of Deucalion" (4.41). There is added interest in this particular case because Celsus combines a philosophical argument with the historical one. He argues that the flood of Noah = Deucalion is but the latest in a series of floods from all eternity. His point is that Noah's flood presupposes a creation in time, whereas according to Celsus the cosmos is eternal (4.79b).

sons, Otus and Ephialtes, to storm Olympus, while Sodom and Gomorrah (Gen. 19:1-29) is derived from the tale of Phaethon's fateful and reckless attempt to drive his father's sun chariot. The story of Adam in paradise (Gen. 2:15–3:24) is likened in its silliness to the deliberately confused statement of the comic poets that Proetus married Bellerophon, etc.[40]

But there is yet another aspect to Celsus' argument. Andresen has argued convincingly that Celsus' attack on Christianity was directed specifically against Justin Martyr and his apologetic theology.[41] Like his refusal to accept allegorical harmonizations of the scriptures with Middle Platonism, so his argument that Moses' cosmogony stems from a misunderstanding of Greek mythology is a simple reversal of Justin's argument that Greek myths resulted from a misunderstanding of the biblical stories. In his *Apology* (*ca.* 155) Justin argues that although the Greeks "heard the words of the prophets they did not understand them accurately" (54). As a specific example he cites the words of "the prophet Moses" about the binding of the colt in Gen. 49:10 and states that the Greeks, in their ignorance of the true meaning of Moses' prophecy, interpreted it to mean that "Bellerophon . . . had gone up to heaven on the horse Pegasus" (*ibid.*). This striking parallel with Celsus (6.49b) suggests that Celsus' *historical* argument may well be a simple reversal of Justin's argument, itself borrowed from prior Jewish apologetic works, that Greek wisdom was derived from the books of Moses.

Moses' Theology of Creation

One basic element of Celsus' *archaios logos* was his understanding of creation, and consequently he devoted considerable attention to a criticism of Moses' cosmogony. Here again his attack is threefold—polemical, historical, and theological:

[Moses' words are considered to be] empty myths not even capable of being interpreted allegorically (1.20b).

[40] For the stories of Proetus, Bellerophon, and Pegasus, see H. J. Rose, *A Handbook of Greek Mythology* (1953 [5]), pp. 270 f.

[41] Andresen, *Logos und Nomos*, pp. 308-400; cf. the approving review of Andresen by A. D. Nock in JTS 7 (1956): 314-17, and the equally positive comments by H. Chadwick, *Early Christian Thought and the Classical Tradition* (1966), pp. 22-24.

Besides, the cosmogony too is very silly (6.49a). . . . Moses and the prophets who left our books had no idea what the nature of the world and of mankind really is, and put together utter trash (6.50).[42]

The polemical intent of these excerpts is evident. Their goal is simply to ridicule Moses and his cosmogony. Origen himself was aware of this, for he protests in 6.50, "If he had stated the reason why he thought the divine scriptures were *utter trash,* we should have tried to demolish the arguments. . . ." In 1.20b Celsus denies that Moses' words are capable of yielding to allegorical interpretation, and in 1.17 he attacks those who treat Moses' cosmogony allegorically. Quite obviously, Celsus' rejection of allegory is dictated by his polemical intentions. Because the Jews have abandoned the *archaios logos,* he argues, there is a priori no deeper wisdom in their account of creation. When he comes to his detailed examination of the Mosiac cosmogony in book 4, he repeats this charge at almost every turn (4.38,48,49,50, and 51). The last passage (4.51) is of special interest because it confirms the view that Celsus refused to accept allegorical interpretations of biblical material under any conditions:

At any rate, the allegories which seem to have been written about them are far more shameful and preposterous than the myths, since they connect with some amazing and utterly senseless folly ideas which cannot by any means be made to fit.

Coupled with the purely polemical and the historical arguments against the Mosaic cosmogony is a theological or philosophical one:

[He asserts that the narrative of Moses represents God] most impiously, making Him into a weakling right from the beginning, and incapable of persuading even one man whom He had formed . . . (4.40).

After this, indeed, God, exactly like a bad workman, was worn out and needed a holiday to have a rest (6.61a).

Nor did he make man his image; for God is not like that, nor does he resemble any other form at all (6.63).

[42] Among the stories which Celsus regarded as utter trash are the story of Lot and his daughters which he describes as "more iniquitous than Thyestian sins" (4.45), and especially the story of Joseph's tribulations which he analyzes at length (4.46-47).

In order for this philosophical attack to succeed, Celsus must rely on his earlier refusal to allow allegorical interpretation. Only by reading Moses' words at their crudest and most anthropomorphic level can he establish the necessary opposition between himself and his opponents. Thus he interprets *katapauein* ("to rest") in Gen. 2:2-3 to mean that God was worn out following his work and strengthens his case by substituting *anapausis*, which normally means to rest from work.[43] With respect to the creation of man, he takes particular delight in ridiculing the notion that God created man in his image and with his own hands, that woman was formed from the man's side, and, worst of all, that a serpent was somehow able to overcome the creator (4.36, 6.61b). Here his argument is not merely that Moses ignored the inspired tales of the ancients (4.36), but more seriously that his conception of the deity, as interpreted by Celsus, violates the principle of divine transcendence as understood by Middle Platonism.[44] The supreme God, Celsus explains in 6.62 ff., is utterly removed from the sphere of human activity and transience, whereas Moses' God appears to him, in Chadwick's words, as a "busy, interfering deity." [45]

Our examination of Celsus' assessment of Moses has shown two rather distinct aspects. On the one hand he seems to show familiarity with the older view of Moses as a wise lawgiver, a view which he rejects outright, and with the tradition of the Egyptian origin of the Jews, which he accepts without question. On the other hand, his main interest is not in Moses as a person but as a philosopher of creation, whose writings had come to form the basis of Christian theology. In this sense, Moses is not his chief opponent, but rather Jesus and the later Christian theologians, who attempted to interpret him for their own purposes. Thus it is probably fair to say that

[43] The fact that Aristobulus, *apud* Eusebius, *Praep. Evang.* 13.12.9 f. (667bc), and Philo, *Leg. All.* 1.5-6, had already emphasized precisely this distinction seems to indicate that Celsus was not the first to accuse the Jewish God of weakness. A similar theme appears in 6.51, where Celsus interprets Gen. 1:3 ("let there be light") to mean that the creator was in darkness and needed to borrow light from a higher and more powerful deity.

[44] On the Middle Platonic understanding of divine transcendence, see Festugière, *Révélation,* 4:92-140, and esp. pp. 115-23 on Celsus.

[45] *Early Christian Thought,* p. 25. Chadwick (26) also suggests that Celsus did not develop these criticisms *ex nihilo,* but that he appropriated some of the arguments used by Marcion against the God of the Jews; cf. Celsus' discussion of the creator god and Marcion in 5.54 and 61 f.

Celsus might never have mentioned Moses at all if Christian theologians had not made him the spokesman for their amalgamation of biblical and Greek thought. But inasmuch as the Jewish legends had been appropriated by this new and dangerous religion, which Celsus recognized as a serious threat to his own classical heritage, he mustered every available argument—polemical, philosophical, and historical—to discredit these legends and above all their author, Moses.

Julian the Emperor

The last pagan writer to deal extensively with Moses is also the last significant political and religious representative of Greek and Roman pagan culture in the ancient world. The Emperor Julian was raised and educated in his early years as a Christian, later studied under Aedesius, Chrysanthius, Maximus of Ephesus, and corresponded with Libanius, all Neoplatonists.[46] But by the time of his proclamation as emperor in 360 he had renounced Christianity entirely in favor of a syncretistic religion which consisted of solar mysticism combined with elements of traditional Greek polytheism.[47]

On Julian's attitude toward the Jews we possess considerable data, scattered here and there among his substantial literary remains. Even if we reject as spurious the letter *To the Community of the Jews*,[48] we know from other writings of his desire to rebuild the temple in Jerusalem.[49] More important yet, we have access to his anti-Christian

[46] On the life of Julian, see J. Bidez, *La vie de l'empereur Julien* (1930; repr. 1965) and the brief survey in *The Works of the Emperor Julian*, ed. and tr. W. C. Wright (LCL) 3 (1923) : vii-xxvi. On the extent of Julian's indebtedness to his Neoplatonic teachers, see P. Labriolle, *La réaction païenne* (1934) , pp. 378-88 and 421-33, and Bidez, *Vie*, pp. 50-81.

[47] M. Nilsson, *Geschichte der griechischen Religion*, 2:458, summarizes Julian's religion as follows: "Seine Theologie, die höhere Gotteserkenntnis der Neuplatoniker, war dem Volk unzugänglich, die Theurgie aber, die sich für die höhere Form der Gottesgemeinschaft ausgab, war verkappte Magie. . . ."

[48] 51 Wright = 204 Bidez; where appropriate, subsequent references to Julian's works will cite the enumeration both of Wright (LCL) and of the Budé volume, *Iuliani Imperatoris epistulae leges poemata fragmenta varia*, ed. J. Bidez and F. Cumont (1922) . For discussions of the famous letter to the Jews, see Wright, *Works* 3, xxii, and J. Vogt, *Kaiser Julian und das Judentum* (1939) , pp. 35 f.

[49] Of Julian's *desire* to rebuild the temple there is no doubt. This is proven by a fragment of an authentic letter to the Jews preserved in Lydus, *Mens.* 4.53: "And Julian the Emperor, when he was fighting the Persians, wrote to the Jews and said the following, 'I am going to rebuild the temple of the highest god with all haste.' " Cf. the discussion in Vogt, *Kaiser Julian*, pp. 46-47.

treatise, *Contra Galileos* (*ca.* 362),[50] large segments of which are preserved in Cyril of Alexandria's bitter reply to Julian, *Pro Christiana religione adversus Iulianum Imperatorem.*[51]

Positively, Julian's evaluation of Judaism expresses itself in two areas—its sense of tradition and adherence to ancient rites, and its god for whom he had high regard:

> But the Jews are in part god-fearing, seeing that they revere a god who is truly most powerful and most good and governs this world of sense, and, as I well know, is worshiped by us also under other names.[52]

His views on the Jewish cult appear most clearly in his letter *To the High Priest Theodorus.*[53] In 453B of this letter he affirms the programmatic belief of Neoplatonism "that we ought to observe the laws that we have inherited from our forefathers. . . ." [54] Then, having deplored the neglect of traditional pagan rites in his own time, he presents the Jews as paradigms of piety:

> For I saw that those whose minds were turned to the doctrines of the Jewish religion are so ardent in their belief that they would choose to die for it rather than taste pork . . . (453D).[55]

[50] As reconstructed from Cyril of Alexandria (see next note) by C. J. Neumann, *Iuliani imperatoris librorum contra Christianos quae supersunt* (1880). Neumann's text is reprinted in Wright, *Works* 3:318-427. For the English translation I have relied exclusively on Wright.

[51] Migne, PG 76. Cyril's reply was written between 433 and 441 c.e. Toward the end of his tenth book, Cyril describes his literary method as follows (315C) : "All of this he [Julian] discusses at great length. But we omit superfluous and foolish arguments and extract only the sense of what he says. We must, I think, contrast the truth with his petty ideas as he strives to demonstrate the futility of Christianity." In other words our picture of Julian's work is far from complete. Apart from the fact that we possess only ten of the twenty or more books in Cyril's original reply, we can assume on the basis of his comments that he omitted extensive sections of Julian's work and that his summaries reflect his deep antipathy for Julian.

[52] *Letter to Theodorus* 453D-454A; cf. *c. Gal.* 354B: "but nevertheless I revere always the god of Abraham, Isaac, and Jacob. . . . And they revered a god who was ever gracious to me and to those who worshiped him as Abraham did, for he is a very great and powerful god. . . ."

[53] 20 Wright = 89a Bidez.

[54] The full statement runs as follows: "I am cautious and I avoid innovation in everything, but especially with respect of the gods"; cf. also *c. Gal.* 238B: "Why is it that you [Christians] do not abide even by the traditions of the Hebrews or accept the law which god has given to them?"

[55] A similar statement is found in Sext. Emp., *Pyr.* 3.24.223: "For a Jew or an Egyptian priest would rather die than eat pork."

102

One particular aspect of the Jewish cult which attracted Julian's attention and admiration was the role of sacrifice.[56] In this he saw a common bond between Judaism and pagan religions which united them over against the nonsacrificing Christians:[57] "Since all the rest we have in a manner in common with them [the Jews]—temples, altars, purifications and certain precepts" (c. Gal. 306B).[58]

On the other side of the ledger, Julian's assessment of the Jews as a people was not entirely favorable. Given his status as heir to the power of Rome and staunch supporter of a pagan revival, his enthusiasm for monotheistic Judaism was necessarily limited. This negative aspect reveals itself in c. Gal. 176 ff. where he addresses a series of criticisms to the Jews as part of his argument against the Jewish belief that they alone were God's chosen people: God has "bestowed on the Hebrews nothing considerable or of great value" (176A-B); he has not enabled them "to originate any science or any philosophical study" (178A); their law is "harsh and stern and contains much that is savage and barbarous" (202A); they have been "free for a short time only and then forever . . . enslaved and aliens" (209D ff.); and finally, politics and learning are "in a miserable and barbarous state among the Hebrews" (221E). In connection with these criticisms several observations are in order. First, Julian did not invent these charges but rather took them over from the common stock of Greek and Roman anti-Jewish polemics, whose intention was to refute the claims of Jewish and Christian apologists concerning the cultural and religious priority of the Jews.[59] Second, as in the case of Celsus and Porphyry,

[56] Vogt, Kaiser Julian, pp. 41 f. notes that sacrifice constituted the very essence of Julian's religion. In his letter To Aristoxenus (35 Wright = 78 Bidez) Julian urges Aristoxenus "to meet me at Tyana . . . and show me a genuine Hellene among the Cappadocians. For I observe that as yet some refuse to sacrifice . . ." (375C); in the letter To Libanius (58 Wright = 98 Bidez) he speaks enthusiastically of his visit to Batnae: "Its name is barbarous but the place is Hellenic; I say so because through all the country round about the fumes of frankincense arose on all sides and I saw everywhere victims ready for sacrifice" (400C).

[57] C. Gal. 305D ff. To Christians who charged that the Jews no longer sacrificed, Julian replies that only the destruction of the temple is to blame and that they replaced actual sacrifices with symbolic substitutes.

[58] Cf. also c. Gal. 356C, where he praises Abraham's skill in sacrifices, divination, and augury: "For Abraham sacrificed just as we, always and continously; and he also prophesied by the shooting stars; this too is probably Hellenic." On Abraham's knowledge of astrology, see Ginzberg, Legends of the Jews, 1:225 and 234 f.

[59] Apparently these apologists were still effective in their work, for Julian excoriates the "wretched Eusebius" who would have it "that poems in hexameter are

103

the criticisms are directed primarily against Christians, who claimed the Jewish scriptures as their own, and only secondarily against Jews.[60] Third, Jews clearly rank ahead of Christians—and just as clearly behind Greeks—in Julian's hierarchy of cultural values. In his letter *To the Alexandrians,* he writes,

> Your founder was . . . Alexander of Macedon, in no way, by Zeus, like any of these persons, nor again did he resemble any Hebrews, though the latter have shown themselves far superior to the Galileans (433C).[61]

Thus Julian's feelings about the Jews must be described as ambivalent. Together with his serious respect for the "patriarchs" of the ancient Hebrews—Abraham, Solomon, and Moses—he regards the Judaism of his own day with a mixture of admiration and disdain.

Moses the Lawgiver

As one would expect, Julian refers to Moses as the lawgiver of the Hebrews and the author of the Pentateuch: "Moreover, he [the creator] sent us also lawgivers in no way inferior to Moses, if indeed many of them were not far superior" (*c. Gal.* 141D). Thus the entire discussion is in fact a debate between Julian the pagan and Moses the Jew.[62] But as lawgiver of the Hebrews, Moses is necessarily relegated to an inferior position in comparison with Greek lawgivers. In 184B, for instance, Julian compares him unfavorably with Plato, Socrates, Thales, and others, and adds the charge that Moses was a cruel general who punished even "those who had done no wrong."[63] Beyond these general terms of reference, it is interesting to note that Julian nowhere refers to Moses in connection with the exodus of the Israelites from Egypt. Indeed, the theme of the exodus, so common in earlier Greek and Roman anti-Jewish literature, appears scarcely two or three times in Julian's writings.

---

to be found among them" and who "sets up the claims that the study of logic exists among Hebrews . . ." (222A) ; cf. *Praep. Evang.* 11.5.7 (514b), where Eusebius says that the "Great Song of Moses" (Deut. 32:1-43; cf. also Exod. 15:1-18) and David's Psalm 118 were written in Greek heroic meter.

[60] Cf. *c. Gal.* 253B: "Now since the Galileans say that . . . they are still, precisely speaking, Israelites in accordance with their prophets and that they obey Moses above all. . . ."

[61] 47 Wright = 111 Bidez.

[62] Julian uses "Jews" and "Hebrews" at will and with no apparent distinction in meaning.

[63] Possibly referring to the slaughter of the Amalekites as recorded in Exod. 17.

While Julian refers elsewhere (202A) to the laws of the Hebrews as harsh and stern, he reserves special praise for the Mosaic decalogue: "That is an admirable law of Moses, I mean the famous decalogue, 'Thou shalt not steal . . .'" (c. Gal. 152B).

He cites Exod. 20:1-16a, presumably because he regards these social injunctions as the epitome of the decalogue, and asks: "Now except for the command Thou shalt not worship other gods, and Remember the sabbath day, what nation is there . . . which does not think that it ought to keep the other commandments" (152C-D). In fact, he adds, these nations have even established penalties for violators, some more severe, some similar to and some more lenient than those fixed by Moses. Thus while he expresses admiration for Moses' formulation of the law, his excision of the two distinctively Hebrew elements in it (monotheism and sabbath) effectively deprives Moses of any claim to originality. Here again the argument seems to be formulated against the background of Jewish and Christian apologists who claimed that Greek lawgivers, and above all Plato, derived their laws *en bloc* from the writings of Moses.

Moses the Theologian

Underlying Julian's dissatisfaction with Moses' theology, but nonetheless curiously not a prominent feature of his arguments as such, is the charge of atheism, i.e., the rejection of polytheism. Although Julian regarded the refusal of the Jews to worship other gods as a serious affront to "true piety," he goes to considerable lengths to disassociate Moses from the Jews in this regard:

Although the lawgiver (Moses) forbade them to serve any god but the one "whose portion is Jacob, and Israel an allotment of his inheritance" [cf. Deut. 32:9], he did not say only this but added, I think, "Thou shalt not revile gods" [Exod. 22:28]. Yet the shamelessness and audacity of later generations . . . has thought that blasphemy accompanies the neglect of worship (c. Gal. 238C).

Again, hear how much he [Moses] says about the apotropaic deities, "And he shall take two he-goats . . ." [cf. Lev. 16:5-8] (c. Gal. 299A).

Thus it is clear from what has been said [Lev. 16:15, "Then he shall kill the he-goat which is for the sin of the people . . ."] that Moses knew the methods of sacrifice (c. Gal. 305B).

105

Julian interprets the injunction of Exod. 22:28 (LXX) as an expression of Moses' respect for pagan deities,[64] and blames later generations, not Moses, for implacable opposition to polytheism. In the same vein, he quotes the account of Babel (Gen. 11:4-8), "Let *us* go down . . . ," as proof that Moses recognized other gods as well (*c. Gal.* 146B). Finally, he regards the prescriptions in Leviticus concerning the day of atonement as proof that Moses knew and followed the established practices of ancient religion. In short, Julian has followed the same path as Strabo and Tacitus in separating Moses, whose legislation is essentially in harmony with acceptable pagan practices, from his successors who introduced blasphemous regulations about the pagan gods.[65]

Julian also examines Moses' creation story in some detail, including an extensive resumé and analysis of Gen. 1:1-18 (beginning in *c. Gal.* 96C) followed by an equally lengthy comparison of Moses and Plato on their respective accounts of creation (49 A-D, 57 B-66A):

Accordingly, since Moses seems to have failed in his attempt to give a complete account of the immediate creator of the universe . . . (*c. Gal.* 99D).

In all this, you observe, Moses does not say that the deep was created by god, or the darkness or the waters. And yet, after saying concerning light that god ordered it to be, and it was, surely he ought to have gone on to speak of night also, and the deep and the waters. But of them he says not a word to imply that they were not already existing at all, though he mentions them. Furthermore, he does not mention the birth or creation of the angels or in what manner they were brought into being, but deals only with the heavenly and earthly bodies. It follows that according to Moses, god is the creator of nothing that is incorporeal, but is only the disposer of matter that already existed. For the words, "And the earth was invisible . . ." [Gen. 1:2] can only mean that he regards the wet and dry substance as the original matter and that he introduces god as the disposer of this matter (*c. Gal.* 49D-E).

[64] LXX Exod. 22:27 has *ou kakologēseis theous* for MT *Elohim lo teqallel*. A similar interpretation of Exod. 22:27 appears in Philo, *Spec. leg.* 1.53. Prof. Wayne Meeks points out to me that the Greek translation probably presupposes an apologetic reply to charges of Jewish sacrilege.

[65] In his discussion of this charge, M. Adler, "The Emperor Julian and the Jews," JQR 5 (1893): 597, exaggerates when he says that atheism was "the head and front of the offending Jews." This is true only if we disassociate Moses from the Jews on this issue.

But if he [Moses] pays first honor to a sectional god, and then makes the lordship of the whole universe contrast with his power, then it is better to believe as we do, and to recognize the God of all, though not without apprehending also the god of Moses; this is better, I say, than to honor one who has been assigned the lordship over a very small portion, instead of the creator of all things (c. Gal. 148C).

Julian's exegesis of the Mosaic cosmogony focuses on three closely related issues: first, Moses' failure to mention the creation of the angels (96C) and the spirit (96E); second, the fact that Moses said "nothing whatsoever about the gods who are superior to this creator" (96C); and third, the precise nature of the creative activity which Moses attributes to his creator (96D-E). In 49D-E he then uses these observations, not to discard the cosmogony as Celsus had done, but rather in a constructive manner to ascertain the precise nature and function of the creator in Moses' account. From Moses' failure to mention the creation of angels and the spirit, i.e., intermediary spiritual beings, he concludes that Moses' god is the "creator of nothing spiritual" (49E). From Moses' silence "about the gods who are superior to this creator" he must have deduced, although the extant fragments do not include this deduction, that Moses' god is not identical with the highest gods in the divine hierarchy. Finally, from the fact that Moses nowhere says that god created the deep, or darkness, or water, i.e., the primordial matter from which the cosmos was created, he arrives at the conclusion that Moses' god is not a creator *ex nihilo* but rather "the disposer of matter that already existed" (49E).

Again, in discussing Moses' account of the confusion of tongues (Gen. 11:4-8), Julian describes it as "wholly mythical" and concludes that the actions attributed by Moses to his god are entirely inappropriate for the highest god (134D-146B). By thus assigning to the creator responsibility for the confusion of languages, Moses makes him a sectional god and "one who has been assigned lordship over a very small portion" (148B). In short, Julian rejects Moses' claim that the god of the Hebrews is the supreme deity and attempts to substantiate his own position through an analysis of Moses' words. Contrary to Celsus, with whose specific criticism he shows occasional affinities,[66]

[66] For a discussion of possible borrowings by Julian from Celsus and Porphyry, see Harnack, *Porphyrius, "Gegen die Christen,"* pp. 32 f., and P. Labriolle, *La réaction païenne,* pp. 421-23.

107

Julian does not reject Moses as a theologian but rather criticizes him and attempts to integrate Moses' theology into his own Neoplatonic system.

Moses, Jesus, and the Christians

It is not surprising that in a treatise against the Christians, Julian should have occasion to speak of Jesus and Moses together, for both were regarded as founders of their respective religions, and Moses was widely interpreted as a model of perfect virtue and a forerunner or type of the Christ in early Christian literature.[67] Thus, his only direct comparison of the two has Moses quite naturally emerge as a superior holy man:

> Moses after fasting forty days received the law [Exod. 34:28] and Elijah after fasting for the same period, was granted to see god face to face [1 Kings 19:8 f.]. But what did Jesus receive after a fast of the same length? (Fr. 2, Wright).[68]

In a rather different confrontation of Moses and Jesus, Julian criticizes the attempt by Christians to discover prophetic references to Jesus and Christianity in the writings of Moses:

> Moses, then, not once or twice or thrice but very many times says that men ought to honor one god only, and in fact names him the highest; but that they ought to honor another god he nowhere says. He speaks of angels and lords, and moreover of several gods, but from these he chooses out the first and does not assume any god as second, either like or unlike him, such as you have invented (c. Gal. 253B-C).

One charge is that Christians have misinterpreted biblical passages. Deut. 18:18 ("The lord your god shall raise up for you a prophet like me from your brethren") does not refer, as Christians claimed, to the son of Mary, and even if it did, the prophet in question is likened to Moses, not to God (253C). Gen. 49:10 ("The power shall not leave Judah nor a leader from his loins") refers not to "the son of Mary" but "to the royal house of David, which, you

---

[67] On the figure of Moses in early Christian writings, see the literature cited above, p. 16, n. 3.

[68] Augustine notes that Moses, Elijah, and Jesus each fasted forty days (Serm. 252.11; Ep. 55.28). These texts suggest that Julian may simply have turned a traditional Moses-Jesus topos into a polemic against Jesus.

observe, came to an end with King Zedekiah" (253D). Again, Num. 24:17 ("A star shall arise out of Jacob and a man out of Israel") "relates to David and to his descendants," not to Jesus (261E). A second charge is that Christians worship two gods, the father and the son, whereas Moses repeatedly forbids the worship of any deity except the one highest God of Israel. To this effect Julian cites Deut. 4:35 and 39; 6:4; 32:39. Against Christians who protest that they do not assert the existence of two or three gods (262B) he quotes their own scriptures, i.e., John 1:18 (". . . and the word was with god and the word was god"). As for the restriction of the term "son of god" to Jesus, Julian objects that Moses calls angels gods (290B-D) and asks why Moses did not mention Jesus when he calls Israel his "only begotten son" (290D-E). Finally, in a fit of outrage, he rejects the argument of Christians that the Jewish scriptures had prophesied the abrogation of the Mosaic law. "That they say this falsely I will clearly show by quoting from the books of Moses not merely ten but ten thousand passages where he says that the law is for all time" (c. Gal. 319D).

Throughout this section dealing with the Christian use and interpretation of Jewish scriptures Julian has sounded very much like the Jewish spokesmen in the Christian *Adversus Judaeos* literature.[69] Although the Jewish side of these dialogues has been played down or eliminated altogether by their Christian authors, enough still remains for us to determine that they consisted largely of exegetical disputes on key biblical passages. Texts such as Deut. 18:18; Num. 24:17, and Gen. 49:10, which Julian quotes, must have figured in these disputes. It is safe to assume, for instance, that Julian's observation about Gen. 49:10, that it was "most certainly not said of the son of Mary" (253C), is a reflection of the Jewish reply to Justin Martyr's exegesis of the same passage in his *Dialogue with Trypho* 120: "And it is plain that this was spoken not of Judah, but of Christ." Similarly, something like Trypho's challenge, ". . . and show us that the spirit of prophecy admits another god besides the maker of all things" (Justin, *Dial.* 55) probably underlies Julian's argument that

[69] See the discussion by M. Freimann, "Die Wortführer des Judentums in den ältesten Kontroversen zwischen Juden und Christen," MGWJ 55 (1911): 555-85; A. B. Hulen, "The 'Dialogues with the Jews' as Sources for the Early Jewish Argument Against Christianity," JBL 51 (1932): 58-70; and A. L. Williams, *Adversus Judaeos* (1935).

the Christians violate the scriptures by worshiping two gods (*c. Gal.* 262B). Finally, the issue of the temporal limits of the Mosaic law was a perennial point of dispute, beginning with Paul and again present in the mind of the Jew Trypho:

> But this is what we are most at a loss about: that you, professing to be pious, and supposing yourselves better than others are not in any particular separated from them . . . in that you observe no festivals, or sabbaths, and do not have the rite of circumcision . . . (Justin, *Dial.* 10).

It has also been noted that Julian must have known earlier pagan attacks on Christianity and incorporated elements of them into his own writing against the Christians. Thus the prominence of Moses in his work is to a large extent inherent in the literary genre which he inherited from earlier critics like Celsus and Porphyry. On one significant point, however, Julian differs from these predecessors. During his early years of study under Christian teachers at Nicomedia and Constantinople, and especially during his six years of seclusion in the castle of Macellum in Cappadocia, he acquired considerable familiarity with the writings of the Old and New Testaments. He quotes passages with ease from either Testament, although his sympathies are distinctly on the side of the Old.[70] In questions of disputed interpretations of Old Testament texts, he sides consistently with Jewish rather than Christian exegesis. In both instances his preference is a clear reflection of his general attitude toward Moses and ancient Judaism.

Can we probe further into the roots of Julian's attitude? Does his sympathy for Moses derive from his appreciation of cultural diversity in ancient religions, from his bitter opposition to Christianity, from a desire to enlist support from the Jews for his campaign against the Persians, or from a combination of such factors? It would be impossible, I think, either to eliminate any of these factors as insignificant or to establish a definite priority among them. His conversion to paganism arose undoubtedly from a real dissatisfaction with Christianity, and this dissatisfaction was subsequently reinforced by the

---

[70] Apart from the Pentateuch, Julian quotes from or refers to the following Old Testament writings: 1 Samuel, 1 Kings, Psalms, Hosea; he also quotes from or refers to the following New Testament writings: Matthew, Mark, Luke, John, Acts, Romans, 1 Corinthians, Colossians, 1 Thessalonians, and Hebrews.

Neoplatonic insistence on the absolute value of "ancient-ness," as well as by the fact that Christians dominated two key cities of the Empire, Antioch and Alexandria. Beyond this, we should not forget that Julian fell heir to a particular type of Neoplatonism which placed great value on non-Greek (including Jewish) wisdom.[71] This complex web of religious, political, and philosophical factors must be kept in mind in any attempt to understand the combination of critical and appreciative elements in Julian's attitude toward Moses.

Conclusion

Among the writers who in various ways regarded Moses as a deficient, and sometimes evil, lawgiver, there are two distinct groups. Both were critical of Moses, but their information, perspective, and motives were entirely different. The first group consists of Latin-writing Romans—Quintilian, Tacitus, and Juvenal—who had no direct knowledge of the Jewish scriptures and whose knowledge of Moses was derived primarily from pagan sources. In the main their image of Moses, as of the Jews generally, was informed by the political struggles between Rome and the Jews that lasted, with but brief respites, from the time of Pompey through the time of Hadrian. The second group differs from the first in practically every respect. It is made up of Greek-writing authors of non-Roman origins—Galen, Celsus, and Julian—who lived at the time when Christianity had begun to assert its presence in the Empire and to supplant Judaism as a source of concern to Rome. This new situation meant that their sources of information were no longer limited to pagan traditions and Jewish apologetic material, but now included biblical material as well. This new source and the way in which Galen, Celsus, and Julian reacted to the more traditional pagan and Jewish picture of Moses produced a new image. The Jewish apologetic material, which had been appropriated by Christian writers, was responsible for the fact that Moses was treated as a philosopher of creation, while at the same time increased knowledge of Jewish scriptures tended to negate the idealizing tendencies inherent in the apologetic literature. Thus Galen, Celsus, and Julian reflect but do not accept the Moses of Strabo, Justin, and the Jewish traditions behind them. Instead, they refer directly to biblical pas-

---

[71] So Vogt, *Kaiser Julian*, p. 36.

sages and, by refusing to accept allegorical interpretations, conclude that Moses was an inferior philosopher of creation in comparison to Plato and the other Greeks. A mitigating factor in their criticisms, however, is the fact that their primary enemy is not Moses but the Christians; no matter how lowly they regarded Moses, they were sure to think even more lowly of the Christians.

3. Moses and the Exodus

In pagan tradition, as in Jewish scriptures, Moses' renown rested not only on his legislation but also on his role in the exodus of the Israelites from Egypt. The biblical version of the exodus expresses tremendous hostility between the people of Yahweh and the people of Pharaoh and expresses it from Israel's point of view. Centuries later, in Ptolemaic Egypt, the people of Egypt enjoyed some measure of revenge in the form of exodus narratives written from the Egyptian point of view. Among pagan writers on the Jews, these stories enjoyed considerable popularity and were widely accepted as authentic accounts of Jewish origins. The chief figure in these stories was Moses, presented not as the ambassador of God and the champion of an unjustly oppressed people, but as one rejected by the gods and opposed to all true religion. The story first appears under the name of Manetho, the well-known Egyptian priest and author of the third century B.C.E., and the last traces of it appear in the little-known Helladius of Antinoupolis some six hundred years later.

Manetho

Shortly after, or perhaps contemporary with, Hecataeus of Abdera (*ca.* 300 B.C.E.) is the account of the exodus attributed by Josephus to the Egyptian author Manetho.[1] Manetho was a native priest of Sebennytus in the Delta who had served as a priest at Heliopolis and played an important role in the official establishment of the Serapis cult under Ptolemy I Soter or Ptolemy II Philadelphus.[2] As an author he is known primarily for his *Aegyptiaca*, fragments of which are preserved by Josephus and later Christian chronographers. In book 1 of his *Contra Apionem* Josephus adduces the testimony of Manetho's *Aegyptiaca* to support two theses against anti-Jewish writers, i.e., the great antiquity of the Jews and their non-Egyptian origin. In the account of Manetho, which Josephus alternately quotes and paraphrases at great length,[3] Moses is mentioned but once, in the concluding paragraph:

> It is said that the priest who laid down for them the constitution and the laws was an Heliopolitan named Osarsiph after the god Osiris in Heliopolis; when he went over to this nation [the Jews] he changed his name and was called Moses (*Ap*.1.250).

In order to comprehend the problems which surround this passage and the enormous literature which it has spawned, it will be necessary to summarize Josephus' full report of Manetho. In *Ap*.1.75-90 he records Manetho's account of the Hyksos, their lowly origin in the East, their domination of Egypt, their expulsion from Avaris and Egypt by Thoummosis, and their flight to Judaea where they founded the city of Jerusalem. From this account Josephus draws his desired conclusion:

> Manetho has thus furnished us with evidence first that we came into Egypt from elsewhere, and second, that we left it at a date so remote in the past that it preceded the Trojan War by nearly a thousand years (1. 104).[4]

---

[1] On Manetho, see R. Laqueur, "Manetho (1)" RE 27 (1928): 1060-1101, and *Manetho*, ed. and tr. W. G. Waddell (LCL, 1940), pp. vii-xiv.

[2] So Plutarch, *De Is. et Os.* 354C-D and 362A.

[3] *Ap*. 1.75-82 is direct quotation; 1.85-90 is paraphrase; 1.94-102, dealing with events in Egypt following the expulsion of the Hyksos, is also direct quotation.

[4] By the first century B.C.E., chronology had become a key apologetic weapon in the disputes between Jews and Greeks. Both of Manetho's exodus stories (*Ap*. 1.103 f., 203-232) place the departure from Egypt in the second millennium B.C.E. A second tradition, preserved by Tatian (*Ad. Graec.* 38) and attributed to Ptolemy of Mendes, places the exodus in the time of the Egyptian king Amosis who is synchronized with the Argive king Inachus. Still a third tradition, represented

114

By thus assuming that Manetho himself had identified the Hyksos with the Jews, Josephus found in Manetho a star witness whose testimony he exploited to the full.

But Manetho reappears in *Ap.* 1.227-250, at great length, this time not as a friendly witness to the antiquity of the Jews but as a dangerously hostile witness to their Egyptian origin. In 228-231 Josephus summarizes his earlier report of Manetho and in 233-250 he relates an entirely new episode, this one involving the expulsion of the impure people under King Amenophis. A King Or desired a vision of the gods and was told by his diviner, another Amenophis, that the wish would be granted only if the king purged the country of all its lepers; the king gathered some 80,000 impure people and sent them to the quarries. The seer, recognizing that some learned priests were included among the lepers and fearing retribution from the gods, predicted that the unclean people, with outside help, would rule Egypt for thirteen years (232-236). Just as the seer had predicated, the lepers took refuge in the city of Avaris, selected a leader called Osarsiph and prepared to wage war on the land, with assistance from the inhabitants of Jerusalem whose ancestors had been expelled from Egypt long ago (237-243). On hearing of the invasion, the new king Amenophis took the sacred objects and fled into Ethiopia. Together with the Solymites, the lepers instituted a reign of terror under the leadership of the native priest Osarsiph, who later changed his name to Moses.[5] Finally, Amenophis and his son Ramses returned from

---

by Lysimachus, Tacitus, and perhaps Apion (below, pp. 122 ff.) placed the exodus in the reign of Bocchoris (eighth century B.C.E.), i.e., more than 800 years later than the date given by Manetho, Ptolemy, and Josephus. This down-dating probably represents a deliberate manipulation of chronology for apologetic purposes to deprive Moses of this valuable claim to antiquity. Finally, Josephus (*Ap.* 2.17) noted that there were others who fixed Moses' date "as they pleased." On the question of chronology as an apologetic tool, see Ben Zion Wacholder, "Biblical Chronology in the Hellenistic World Chronicles," HTR 61 (1968): 451-81 (esp. pp. 477 ff. on antisemitic chronologies).

[5] Osarsiph has been interpreted by some, notably Tcherikover (*Hellenistic Civilization*, p. 363), as an Egyptianized form of Joseph, in which the Osar- (Osiris) has replaced the Jo- (Iao). This interpretation entails a complicated string of assumptions, e.g., that this Egyptianized name of Joseph was mistakenly applied to Moses, which renders it unlikely and unnecessary. Furthermore, Waddell, *Manetho*, p. 125, n. 3, and J. Marquart, "Chronologische Untersuchungen," *Philologus* Suppl. 7 (1899): 672, agree that it is simply an Egyptian personal name.

Ethiopia with a large army and routed the shepherds (= Hyksos) and their impure friends to the frontiers of Syria (243-251).

From Josephus' point of view this second episode posed a serious threat to his earlier conclusion in that it represented the Jews "as mixed up with a crowd of Egyptian lepers who for various maladies were condemned . . . to banishment from the country" (229). For this reason he undertakes an extensive refutation of it and concludes that this second account is a slanderous fiction derived from "unauthenticated legends." Only the first account (75-90), he says, which Manetho derived from the sacred records is worthy of acceptance as authentic history.

The obvious question, which has long taxed students of Manetho, is whether we can safely attribute to him everything which Josephus reports in his name. Since E. Meyer's work on Egyptian chronology in 1904, there has existed a general consensus that the text of Manetho underwent serious and repeated revisions subsequent to its original publication. While the precise extent of these interpolations has been a subject of considerable debate, Meyer and most others have argued that the references to the Jews and Jerusalem stem not from Manetho himself but from later interpolators.[6]

Whether or not one accepts Meyer's view regarding the inauthenticity of Manetho's fragments in Josephus, there is general agreement that the underlying stories themselves, of which there were many versions (the invasion of Egypt by outsiders, variously called Hyksos and Syrians; the reign of terror under these outsiders who devastated the holy places of the indigenous Egyptian religion; the expulsion of the outsiders by a hero-king), reach far back into Egyptian history and that their application to the Jews is a secondary phenomenon.[7]

---

[6] *Aegyptische Chronologie*, pp. 71-79; Waddell, *Manetho*, pp. xvii-xix; Jacoby, FGH 3C:84. The only serious dissent to this consensus has come from R. Weill, *La fin du moyen empire égyptien* (1918), pp. 70-76 and 101, and V. Tcherikover, *Hellenistic Civilization*, pp. 362 f. Weill's basic argument is that fusion of Jewish and Egyptian elements which is characteristic of Manetho *apud* Josephus was already present in Manetho's predecessor Hecataeus. This would undermine Meyer's argument that Manetho *could* not have referred to the Jews in his history of Egypt.

[7] The long and complicated literary history of these tales is discussed by Weill, *La fin du moyen empire*, pp. 22-68, 76-83, 111-45, 605-23; cf. also Marquart "Chronologische Untersuchungen," pp. 667-73, and the excellent article of J. Yoyotte, "L'Egypte ancienne et les origines de l'antijudasme," *Bulletin de la Société Ernest*

Once made, however, the identification of the Jews with the invaders became a permanent fixture in Alexandrian literature. Thus the crimes attributed in 238 to Osarsiph:

By his first law he [Osarsiph] ordained that they should not worship the gods nor abstain from the flesh of any of the animals held in special reverence in Egypt, but should kill and consume them all, and that they should have no connection with any save members of their own confederacy. After laying down these and a multitude of other laws, absolutely opposed to Egyptian custom . . . ,

and in 249 to the followers of Osarsiph:

Not only did they set cities and villages on fire, not only did they pillage the temple and mutilate the images of the gods, but, not content with that, they habitually used the very sanctuaries as kitchens for roasting the venerated sacred animals, and forced the priests and prophets to slaughter them and cut their throats, and then turned them out naked . . . ,

were transferred to Moses and became part and parcel of the Alexandrian Moses tradition which appears not only in Alexandrian writers but in Diodorus Siculus and Tacitus as well.

As for the mention of Moses in 250, all agree that it must be regarded as a later addition to Manetho's text. It is pointed out that Osarsiph is mentioned earlier in 238 with no mention of Moses, that the names are spelled differently in 238 and 250,[8] and that the introductory phrase, "it is said that," bears the mark of a secondary comment. Thus 250 seems to be introduced as if in ignorance of 238, where such a comment would normally be expected.

The content of 250 is similar to the statement in Strabo (above, p. 38) that Moses was one of the Egyptian priests and held a part of lower Egypt. The idea that Moses was an Egyptian priest seems to have been fairly widespread, appearing also in Pompeius Trogus and the Jewish apologist Artapanus where it expresses no hostility toward Moses. Only when the idea was adapted and added to the story of

---

Renan, published in RHR 163 (1963): 133-43. For translations of the Egyptian documents which preserve these traditions, cf. *Ancient Near Eastern Texts Relating to the Old Testament*,[2] ed. J. Pritchard (1955), pp. 231-34, 260. On the Hyksos, see J. von Seters, *The Hyksos, A New Investigation* (1966).

[8] In 238 the name occurs as *Osarsiphos* and in 250 as *Osarsiph* (i.e., undeclined).

117

the impure exiles and their leader Osarsiph did it take on the un-
friendly tone which provoked Josephus' invective in 253 and 279-286.
In its present form, according to which Manetho himself is credited
with the identification of Moses and Osarsiph, the material in 250
must be assigned to an anonymous anti-Jewish Alexandrian writer
(hereafter referred to as Ps-Manetho) who wished to claim Manetho's
authority for the account as a whole. As for the date of the interpolation, one possibility is the period around 40 c.e., when Apion and
Chaeremon put together their versions of the exodus. On the other
hand, earlier versions, with explicit mention of Moses, appear in
Lysimachus and Apollonius Molon (first cent. b.c.e.) and in Diodorus Siculus.

Lysimachus

Sometime between the second century b.c.e. and the early first century c.e.,[9] Lysimachus of Alexandria produced a somewhat different
version of the exodus story,[10] which is based on a variant form of
the ancient Egyptian legends. Like the account of Manetho, it has been
adapted secondarily to denigrate Moses and the Jews by showing that
their ancestors were polluted exiles from Egypt:

> On the next day a certain Moses advised them to abandon caution and to
> follow one road until they came to inhabited regions; he exhorted them to
> show kindness to no one, to offer the worst rather than the best advice and
> to overthrow temples and altars of gods whenever they came upon them
> (Josephus, *Ap.* 1.309).

Lysimachus' version differs from Manetho's in that the king at
the time of the exile is Bocchoris,[11] and that the oracle of Ammon has
replaced the diviner as the source of the command to purge the land
of the lepers and other impure people. Moses is not identified as an
Egyptian priest, and the account of his leadership is at once more

[9] On Lysimachus' date, see A. Gudemann, "Lysimachos (20)," RE 27 (1928):
32 ff.
[10] *Apud* Josephus, *Ap.* 1.304-311.
[11] That Bocchoris' name is not an arbitrary substitution is evident from the
observation by Weill, *La fin du moyen empire,* p. 142, that there existed in Hellenistic Egypt a "cycle de Bokchoris" to which the exodus story was attached; cf.
also Yoyotte, "L'Egypte ancienne," p. 138.

118

extensive and more antipathetic. But Lysimachus shares with Ps-Manetho the same basic attitude as well as similar material. The statement that Moses instructed his people to show goodwill to no one and to offer the worst rather than the best advice recalls the comment of Ps-Manetho that Moses forbade his followers to associate with any except members of their own group (Josephus, *Ap*. 1.238). Related to this is *Ap*. 2.145 where Josephus reports the accusations of Apollonius Molon (see above, p. 19), Lysimachus, "and others," who

mainly from ill will have made reflections . . . upon our lawgiver Moses and his code, maligning the one as a charlatan and impostor (*hos goēta kai apateōna*) and asserting that from the other we receive lessons in vice and none in virtue. . . .

To be sure, it is not possible to determine from the text whether Molon and/or Lysimachus used the precise phrase *hos goēta kai apateōna* of Moses. 2.145 may well represent Josephus' own summary of their general attitude rather than of any specific pronouncements. But in either case we know enough of their respective views of Judaism so that we can accept 2.145 as reasonably reflecting also their view of Moses.[12]

The second statement, that Moses advised the people to overthrow temples and altars of the gods, is a specific example of widespread charges of Jewish atheism. In this particular case the expulsion legend reveals itself as the immediate source and origin of the charge. The charge of Jewish sacrilege is nowhere attested in pagan writings apart from the exodus legends, while the theme of hostility toward the indigenous population and religion served as the focal point in the Egyptian expulsion stories long before they were transferred to the Jews. As the Hyksos and the Asians had been accused at an earlier time of impiety toward the gods, so the same charges were attached to Moses and the Jews at a later time when the Jews replaced the Hyksos and the Syrians in the legend as the real or supposed enemies

[12] On Molon's view of Judaism, cf. *Ap*. 2.148: "Apollonius . . . has scattered accusations here and there, sometimes reviling us as atheists and misanthropes and sometimes reproaching our cowardice and in other places, quite to the contrary, he accuses us of rashness and foolish abandon. He says that we are the least gifted of the barbarians and that for this reason we alone have contributed no discovery to civilization." In 2.79 Josephus accuses Molon and Poseidonius together of "telling lies and inventing illogical blasphemies about our temple."

119

of Egypt.[13] This process is especially evident in the account of Ps-Manetho which, as we have seen, had nothing at all to do with the Jews in its original form. The fact that Osarsiph $=$ Moses' program turns up in very similar form in Lysimachus, this time explicitly attributed to Moses, tends to confirm our view that the expulsion story itself, in its pre-Mosaic form, is the source for the themes of sacrilege and misanthropy in Moses' advice to his people.

Chaeremon

The next phase in the Alexandrian expulsion legend is represented by Chaeremon and his contemporary, Apion. Chaeremon, with whom we shall deal first, is known variously as a Stoic philosopher, a *hierogrammateus* ("priestly scribe"), and the author of an *Aigyptiakē Historia* in which he recorded his version of the exodus.[14] Prior to H. I. Bell's publication of Claudius' letter to the Alexandrians,[15] the only evidence for his date were two passages in Suidas, one of which refers to him as the tutor of Nero and the other as the teacher and predecessor of Dionysius of Alexandria, presumably as head of the Museum in Alexandria.[16] These references enable us to place him somewhat before the middle of the first century c.e. With the publication of Claudius' letter, it became known that a Chaeremon, the son of Leonidas, was part of the official delegation sent to Rome in 41 c.e. to congratulate the Emperor Claudius on his accession to power. Inasmuch as Chaeremon's account of the exodus is best understood against the background of the anti-Jewish riots at Alexandria in 38-40, to which Claudius addresses himself in the same letter, it has been assumed that the two Chaeremons are one and the same.[17]

---

[13] The same point is made by Yoyotte, "L'Egypte ancienne," p. 141: "Il serait amusant de comparer certains leitmotive pharaoniques et un choix d'expressions employées dans le monde romain à propos des Juif: 'impies', 'ennemis des dieux' . . . . En Egypte le thème de l'ennemi fut employé à toutes fins utiles: par les Egyptiens contre les Perses puis contre les Grecs . . . mail il semblerait, en fin de compte, que le malheureux peuple d'Israël fut le seul à endosser définitivement, au début de notre ère, cette livrée polyvalente."

[14] On Chaeremon, see E. Schwartz, "Chaeremon (7)," RE 6 (1899): 2025-27, and Jacoby, FGH 3C:145 f.

[15] *Jews and Christians in Egypt* (1924), pp. 23-26; cf. pp. 27-37 for Bell's translation and commentary on the letter. The letter has also been published, with translation and commentary, in CPJ 2:36-55.

[16] So Schwartz, "Chaeremon," pp. 2025 f.

[17] So Bell, *Jews and Christians*, p. 29, and CPJ 2:44.

In *Ap.* 1.288-292, immediately following his final refutation of Manetho, Josephus presents Chaeremon's narrative of the exodus:

He states that Isis appeared to Amenophis in a dream and blamed him for the destruction of her temple during a battle. A sacred scribe Phritobautes told him that his anguish would cease if he cleansed Egypt of its unclean population. He collected 250,000 infected people and expelled them. They were led by scribes, Moses and Joseph, the latter of whom was also a sacred scribe. Their Egyptian names were Tisithen for Moses and Peteseph for Joseph (*Ap.* 1.288-290).

Chaeremon's account is closely related to the version of Ps-Manetho in 230-251. The same basic structure underlies both: the kings involved are Amenophis and Ramses; the strange abandoned army (291), which joined with the exiles in overrunning Egypt, represents the last, confused vestige of the two different accounts in Manetho; and in both, Moses is an Egyptian priest. At the same time there are also significant differences: the name of the scribe is Phritobautes in Chaeremon but Amenophis in Manetho (235); the motive for expulsion is Isis' anger in Chaeremon but the king's desire for a vision of the gods in Manetho (232); and the number of exiles is different in each. As for Moses, his Egyptian name is Tisithen in Chaeremon but Osarsiph in Manetho. In Chaeremon, and here only, Moses and Joseph, both represented as *hierogrammateis*,[18] are co-leaders of the exile. Finally, unlike Manetho and Lysimachus, nothing is said of Moses except that he was co-leader of the exiles. In view of these divergencies we cannot regard either version as directly dependent on the other. Rather they appear to be variant forms of similar Egyptian expulsion stories adapted for similar ends and in a common milieu by the insertion of references to Jewish history.[19] The similar end is anti-Jewish polemic, and the common milieu is Alexandria where Moses was known as an Egyptian priest.

[18] As noted above, p. 120, Chaeremon himself was known as a *hierogrammateus*. According to Liddell-Scott-Jones, *s.v.*, the term designates "a lower order of the Egyptian priesthood."

[19] An interesting parallel to Chaeremon's version is preserved in a papyrus fragment of the third century c.e., published and discussed in CPJ 3:119-21 (no. 520). Like Chaeremon the fragment speaks of Isis' anger at the Jews(?) who may have desolated the land and who must be thrown out of Egypt.

121

The Egyptian names assigned to Joseph[20] and Moses do not occur in any other version of the exodus, nor are they otherwise attested, so far as I have been able to determine, as Egyptian personal names. Whatever their ultimate origin, it is evident that as in the account of Ps-Manetho, so here the names Moses and Joseph belong to the stage of secondary expansion when the story was adapted to the Jews. The extent of this adaptation is slight and the original form of the story readily visible. By the simple removal of Moses and Joseph in 290 and of the single reference to the Jews in 292, we can reconstruct the indigenous Egyptian version as it probably existed centuries before Chaeremon's time.

Apion

Chaeremon's contemporary in Alexandria was Apion, the grammarian and bitter foe of the Alexandrian Jewish community in the third and fourth decades of the first century.[21] Josephus informs us that he was one of the Alexandrian delegates who appeared before the Emperor Caligula in the hearings which arose from the anti-Jewish riots of 38 C.E. (*AJ* 18.257). From Suidas (*s.v. Apion*) we also know that he was the successor to Theon the grammarian, presumably as leader of the Museum. In both respects his career parallels that of Chaeremon. Both were prominent Alexandrian grammarians and both served as official delegates of the city before the Roman emperor at a time when the "Jewish question" was the first order of business in Alexandria. Thus we may conclude that they were not only contemporaries but close professional associates as well.

Like his Alexandrian predecessors, Apion also wrote an *Aegyptiaca* in which he included a version of the exodus.[22] In *Ap* 2.10-11 Josephus records a brief excerpt from this version:

[20] According to Marquart, "Chronologische Untersuchungen," p. 672, Joseph's supposed Egyptian name *Peteseph* means "he whom the god Seph has given"; cf. the name Osar*siph* in *Ap.* 1.238 etc.

[21] On Apion, see L. Cohn, "Apion (3)," RE 2 (1894): 2803-6; Schürer, 3:538-44; Jacoby, FGH 616 (3C:122-26). Apion was best known as a specialist on Homer and traveled throughout Greece as a lecturer on Homer. His efforts prompted the Emperor Tiberius to dub him *cymbalum mundi* (Pliny, HN proem.25). Pliny himself called him *propriae famae tympanum (ibid.)*.

[22] According to Tatian, *Ad Graec.* 38, the work included five books in all. From Josephus' words in *Ap.* 2.5-7 it would appear that anti-Jewish polemic was a main theme in his *Aegyptiaca*.

Moses, as I have heard from the *presbyteroi* of Egypt, was an Heliopolitan; he was bound to the customs of his country and set up open air places of prayer in the various sections of the city and oriented them toward the East, for Heliopolis faced in the same direction. In place of obelisks he set up columns under which a base (*skaphē*) was sculptured; the shadow cast by the sculpture on the base followed the regular course of the sun in the sky (*Ap.* 2.10-11).[23]

Unfortunately, Josephus has included only those "details added by Apion" (2.9). The full account must have been rather lengthy and included details from the common tradition, e.g., Moses as an Egyptian priest, as the leader of the polluted exiles, and as the founder and lawgiver of the Jews as a people. Like Manetho (1.229), Apion claims to have derived his information from Egyptian traditions, "from the *presbyteroi* of the Egyptians."[24] Like Ps-Manetho he identifies Moses as Heliopolitan, although he makes no explicit mention of his priestly office.

The excerpt itself appears to be a description of Moses' role as the founder of the temple cult in Jerusalem, although the details of 2.10-11 are far from clear. Thus the "customs of his country (*patria ethē*)" to which Moses was bound would be the practices of his native Egyptian religion which he adopted as the basis of the new cult in Jerusalem.[25] The account would seem to presuppose that Moses had been a priest at Heliopolis and that he transferred his priestly knowledge from his homeland (Egypt) to his new location in Jerusalem. If this interpretation is correct, Apion's account takes on a rather distinctive color in comparison with Lysimachus and Chaeremon. Whereas the other Alexandrian versions of the exodus dwell on Moses' implacable opposition to Egyptian religion, Apion established it as the very basis of the new cult in Jerusalem. Assuming that Apion was familiar with the tradition of Moses' hostility to Egyptian religion, we can only speculate that he introduced the material of 2.10-11 in order to malign the Jews by portraying the Mosaic cult as an offshoot of Egyptian religion.

One further detail in Josephus' account of Apion suggests that

---

[23] On the textual problems of the passage, see the apparatus in Jacoby, FGH 3C:127 *ad loc.*

[24] Quite possibly Apion used *presbyteroi* to designate a group of civic or cultic officials rather than old people, as Josephus interprets it in 2.13.

[25] So Jacoby, FGH 3C:127 *ad loc.*

123

the Alexandrian may have known more about Moses than the information contained in Egyptian propaganda.[26] From 2.25 it is apparent that Apion knew of Moses' ascent on Mount Sinai:

This amazing Apion, after stating that they came to Judaea after six days, says elsewhere that Moses went up into the mountain called Sinaios, which is between Egypt and Arabia, hid there forty days, and then came down and gave the Jews their laws (*Ap.* 2.25).

As it stands, Apion's information is correct, although his statement that Moses hid for forty days probably represents an interpretation *in sensu malo* of the statement in Exod. 24:16-18 that a cloud covered Moses and Yahweh on the mountain. This raises the question whether Apion knew the story of Moses on Sinai from reading Exodus or whether the information came to him indirectly through whatever channels. It is not impossible that in his capacity as an official of the Museum he was familiar with the Septuagint, but this remains nothing more than a possibility. It should also be noted that Moses' sojourn on the mountain is a fairly frequent theme in the magical papyri (see below, pp. 142 ff.).

Diodorus Siculus

We come now to the influence of the Alexandrian exodus tradition beyond the geographical limits of Egypt. The earliest example of this influence is a fragment from Diodorus Siculus (34.1), preserved in Photius' *Bibliotheca* (244; p. 379, ed. Bekker). The passage reports the advice given to Antiochus VII Sidetes by his counselors during his siege of Jerusalem in *ca.* 134 B.C.E.:

They presented their [the Jews'] ancestors as impious people, hated by the gods, who had been chased from the whole of Egypt. Their bodies covered with leprosy, they were gathered together, as people under a curse, and cast beyond the boundaries [of the country? the temples?] for the purpose of purification.[27]

---

[26] One bit of this propaganda is Apion's anti-Jewish etymology of the word sabbath. In *Ap.* 2.21 Josephus reports that Apion derived it from *sabbo*, an Egyptian word for the disease of the groin which the Jews developed during their six-day march through the desert.

[27] Among the different versions of the Alexandrian tradition, Diodorus stands closest to Lysimachus. They share the specific mention of leprosy and the need to

After describing the strange customs of the Jews and their hatred toward other people, the counselors continue their harangue by citing an incident which purportedly took place during the earlier siege of Jerusalem by Antiochus IV Epiphanes:

When Antiochus, also called Epiphanes, was making war against the Jews he entered the sacred shrine of god, where only the priest is allowed to go. In it he found a stone image of a thick bearded man seated on an ass and holding a book in his hand. He assumed that it was a statue of Moses who founded Jerusalem, brought together the people and in addition laid down for the Jews misanthropic and outrageous customs (Diod. Sic. 34.1).

As in the Alexandrian tradition, Moses is here represented as the founder of Jerusalem and the lawgiver responsible for the misanthropic and strange customs of the Jews. While there is no specific reference to his leadership at the time of the exodus, the tradition is visible in the phrase "who founded Jerusalem and brought together the people." With these traditional elements Diodorus' account has coupled a modified version of the widespread notion that the Jews worshiped an ass or the head of an ass.[28] In comparison with the other versions, Diodorus' is the only one which mentions Moses, and its tone is noticeably less hostile.[29] E. Bickermann has pointed out that it expresses little more than the normal Greek expectation that

purify the country by expelling the lepers, the forceful capture of Judaea, and the resolve of the Jews to show goodwill to no one. Lacking in Diodorus is the name of the king, the command of the oracle, the etymology of Jerusalem, and the mention of Moses as the leader of the exile.

[28] The story occurs in various forms in different authors. According to Apion (apud Josephus, Ap. 2.112-114), Mnaseas (second cent. B.C.E.) told of a certain Zabidus who, during a war between the Jews and the Idumaeans, made his way into the temple and carried off a golden head of an ass. Apion himself (Ap. 2.80) records a version of the tale in his polemic against the Jews: "In this sanctuary Apion dares to assert that the Jews set up the head of an ass, worshipping it and regarding it with great awe." A certain Damocritus (Suidas, s.v.) whose date is unknown, wrote that "the Jews worshipped the head of an ass." Tacitus (Hist. 5.4) relates that while in the desert Moses followed an ass to a source of water (see below, p. 127) and that for this reason the Jews dedicated a statue of an ass in the temple. Plutarch (Quaest. conv. 4.5.2) says that the Jews honor the ass because it brought them to water. The charge of ass worship was subsequently transferred to the Christians; cf. Tert. Apol. 16; Min. Fel., Octav. 9. For a discussion of the legends, see Tcherikover, Hellenistic Civilization, pp. 365 f., and E. Bickermann, "Ritualmord und Eselskult," MGWJ 71 (1927): 255 ff.

[29] Among the versions listed in the preceding note, that of Diodorus stands closest to Apion's. The significant common bond is that both accounts attribute the discovery of the ass in the temple to Antiochus IV.

the founder and lawgiver of a given nation should receive special honors, perhaps even cultic recognition, from his people.[30]

Diodorus' source is not mentioned. Bickermann believes that the story came from Poseidonius[31] and suggests further that his high estimation of Judaism led him to replace a cruder story of Jewish ass worship with the mitigated version of Moses seated on the ass. The chief stumbling block to this and any other pro-Jewish interpretation of Poseidonius is that the only explicitly attested statement on the matter presents him as distinctly hostile toward Judaism. This is the judgment of Josephus in *Ap.* 2.79:

> I am no less amazed at the proceedings of those who supplied him [Apion] with his material, I mean Poseidonius and Apollonius Molon. On the one hand they blame us for not worshipping the same gods as other people, and on the other hand they tell lies and invent illogical blasphemies about our temple. . . .

In discussing Antiochus IV Epiphanes' motives for raiding the temple, Josephus mentions several authors who had previously raised the same issue—Polybius, Strabo, Nicolaus of Damascus, Timagenes, Castor the chronicler, and Apollodorus. Any one of these authors might have transmitted the story. Poseidonius is not mentioned at all, although it is certainly possible to infer from Josephus' notice cited above (*Ap.* 2.79) that Poseidonius also knew and recorded the story of the ass in the temple.

In light of these reservations we can only say that Diodorus has either transmitted or concocted a version of the story which differs in one significant respect from other known versions. Instead of the head of an ass, the focus of the story is a man, whom Antiochus supposed to be Moses, seated on an ass. That this represents a deliberate alteration of an earlier story is very much in doubt. Certain is that the account of Diod. Sic. 34.1 is a conflation of two traditions, the story of the exodus which is definitely of Alexandrian origin and the tale of the ass in the temple which is probably so.[32]

---

[30] E. Bickermann, "Eselskult," p. 260.

[31] "Eselskult," p. 260.

[32] Concerning the date of the material, it probably arose between *ca.* 170 and 129 B.C.E., i.e., the period of the Maccabean rebellion and the early Hasmonean dynasty, for it reflects a time of serious conflict between Seleucids and Jews such as characterized these turbulent years.

Tacitus

The last extensive version of the Alexandrian expulsion story in pagan literature occurs in Tacitus' excursus on the Jews (see above, pp. 82 ff.) in the *Histories:*

Most authors agree that during a plague in Egypt which disfigured bodies, King Bocchoris consulted the oracle of Hammon in search of a remedy and was instructed to purge the kingdom and to deport this race, which was hateful to the gods, into other lands. Thus they were sought out, gathered together and then abandoned in the desert. While most were overcome with tears, one of the exiles, Moses, exhorted them not to expect any help from gods or men, for they were deserted by both, but rather to rely on themselves and to consider as a heavenly guide whoever should first aid them in overcoming their present difficulties. Ignorant of everything they agreed and set out on their uncertain path. They were distressed more by lack of water than anything else and they had fallen over the plain, close to panic, when a herd of wild asses moved from their fodder to a rock that was shaded by a tree. Moses followed them and noticing the grassy terrain uncovered large water veins. This provided relief. They continued for six days and on the seventh day they seized lands, having expelled the natives, and dedicated a city and a temple (*Hist.* 5.3).

The points of contact with the Alexandrian accounts preserved by Josephus are obvious. With Lysimachus (see above, pp. 118 ff.) it shares the following motifs: King Bocchoris, the consultation of the oracle of Ammon, Ammon's command to purge the land by expelling the impure people, the expulsion into the desert, the leadership and encouragement given to the exiles by Moses, and the alien religious practices instituted by him. With Apion's version (above, pp. 122 ff.) Tacitus shares the six-day march and the ass worship in the temple. From these extensive parallels it is apparent that Tacitus must have derived the material of 5.3 from Alexandrian anti-Jewish literature. Thus while "most authors" may include non-Alexandrian authors as well, its primary reference is undoubtedly to the likes of Lysimachus and Chaeremon whose work he probably knew through the intermediary of Apion.[33] But just as Tacitus asserted his inde-

[33] Of these authors it is most likely that Tacitus would have known Apion, who was a well-known figure in Rome during the first century c.e. He was known to and quoted by Pliny the Elder (HN praef. 25) who in turn is quoted by

pendence of his predecessors in his assessment of Moses' legislation, so here his report of Moses in the desert does not conform entirely to the Alexandrian accounts. Moses emerges as the hero of the exodus and is carefully set apart from and above his confused followers. At the same time he has placed relatively more emphasis than his predecessors on the period in the desert as the focal point of Moses' activity. There Moses provided unity and inspiration when the exiles had abandoned themselves to weeping; there he exhorted them to rely on themselves rather than on men and gods who had led them to the point of death; and there his cleverness brought them to unexpected sources of water when they were about to die of thirst.

One problem remains. As a leading politician and historian, and as an official in the college of the *quindecimviri,* Tacitus probably possessed at least a secondhand knowledge of the accounts of Moses in Strabo, Diodorus Siculus, and Pompeius Trogus. If this assumption is correct, why did he choose the one rather than the other? One answer might be that Tacitus simply records the Alexandrian version as the *communis opinio* of his time, as it undoubtedly was. But this reply fails to do justice to the prominence of the account in the excursus as a whole. More adequate, I think, is H. Lewy's proposal that Tacitus' purpose in writing the excursus was to explain to his readers, for whom the bitter struggle of 70 C.E. was not yet a dead memory, the rebellious political character of the Jews; that he saw the roots of this rebelliousness in their religious institutions; and that the Alexandrian account of the exodus symbolized vividly and explained historically their resentment and hatred of everything foreign.[34] At the same time, Lewy's proposal clarifies Moses' role in the excursus, where he symbolizes, as their founder, the rebellious and hostile personality of the Jews. For the Alexandrians, and to a lesser extent for Tacitus, resentment of the Jews was projected backward into history and focused on the figure of Moses whom they regarded as responsible for the evils of later Judaism.

Tacitus in *Hist.* 3.28; cf. Reinach, *Textes,* p. 304, n. 1 and I. Levy, "Tacite," pp. 339 f. (cited above, p. 83, n. 7).

[34] "Tacitus on the Origin and Manners of the Jews," pp. 9 ff. (cited above, p. 83, n. 7). Lewy disputes the traditional interpretation of Tacitus' excursus of the Jews as a typical example of historical ethnography. He claims that Tacitus must have known a great deal about contemporary Judaism and that his choice of the Alexandrian tradition was a deliberate move on his part.

Nicarchus, Ptolemy Chennos, Helladius[35]

Further evidence that the Alexandrian version of the exodus was widely known among pagan authors is provided by Nicarchus the son of Ammonius (date uncertain), Ptolemy Chennos of Alexandria (*fl. ca.* 100 C.E.), and Helladius of Antinoupolis (*fl. ca.* 310 C.E.). These three authors have preserved an alphabetic-etymological tradition according to which Moses was called *alpha* because his body was covered with *alphoi* ("leprous spots"):

Nicarchus—Alpha: the head of a bull is called this by the Phoenicians, and Moses the lawgiver is also called this by the Jews because he had many leprous spots on his body. But Nicarchus the son of Ammonius uttered this nonsense in his book *On the Jews.*[36]

Ptolemy Chennos—Uttering this nonsense the mythographer [Ptolemy] says that Moses, the lawgiver of the Hebrews, was called *alpha* because he had leprous spots on his body.[37]

Helladius—This one too utters the nonsense that Moses was called *alpha* because his body was bespeckled with leprous spots, and he cites Philo as a witness to this falsehood.[38]

[35] For a slightly modified version of this section, see my article, "Moses and Alpha," JTS 20 (1969) : 245-48.

[36] The text occurs in an anonymous Byzantine lexicon, first published by I. Bekker (*Anecdota Graeca* [1814]; see vol. 1, p. 381), and later, using other manuscripts, by L. Bachmann (*Anecdota Graeca,* 1 [1828]: 1-422) ; cf. Jacoby, FGH 3C, pt. 2, pp. 691 f. For a discussion of the lexicon, see L. Cohn, *Griechische Lexicographie,* Appendix to K. Brugmann-A. Thumb, *Griechische Grammatik* (1913 ⁴), p. 699.

[37] Photius, *Bibl.* 190 (p. 151b.9, ed. Bekker). Fragments of Ptolemy's *Kainē* [*Paradoxos* in Suidas] *Historia,* an uncritical collection of diverse mythological and paradoxological material, are preserved by Photius, *Bibl.* 190. The fragment concerning Moses occured in Book 5 as part of a series in which the names of various persons and places are related, in alphabetical order, to the letters of the alphabet. The series probably covered the full alphabet, although Photius' excerpt gives only selections of the first half. For each letter except *alpha* Ptolemy cites only one name; for *alpha* he first cites the river Alpheios and then Moses. From this it would appear that Ptolemy inserted the Moses-saying into the list as an additional example. On Ptolemy, see A. Dihle, "Ptolemaios (77) ," RE 46 (1959) : 1862.

[38] Photius, *Bibl.* 279 (p. 529b.27, ed. Bekker). Helladius the grammarian wrote a number of works in iambic trimeter, among them a Chrestomathy of which Photius, *Bibl.* 279, preserves fragments in prose. The saying about Moses is the first item in Photius' excerpt. On Helladius, see A. Gudemann, "Helladios (2) ," RE 15 (1912) : 98-103.

That the three accounts stem from a common literary tradition is evident. The only signficant variant between Nicharchus and Ptolemy Chennos is the use of *Ioudaioi* in the former and *Hebraioi* in the latter to designate the Jews.[39] Helladius' version shows rather more verbal peculiarities and includes the additional element of claiming support for the tradition from Philo. But the three share the same basic elements (*Mōsēs, kaleisthai, alpha, alphoi, sōma*),[40] and the apparent divergencies of Helladius may be nothing more than his own elaboration of the material. Although no date is known for Nicarchus, he probably antedates Ptolemy and Helladius who were collectors rather than creators of such traditions. Whether Nicarchus himself created the tradition and whether Helladius borrowed his material directly from Ptolemy are questions which cannot be answered on the basis of present evidence.

The tradition itself includes two elements: the cognomen *alpha* as applied to Moses, and its etymological explanation in terms of *alphos*. The second element is clear enough. It derives from the Alexandrian exodus tradition which affirmed that the Jews were expelled because they were lepers. The first element is less transparent. Nowhere in pagan, Christian, or Jewish literature is Moses called *alpha*. Beyond this we must ask whether the cognomen *alpha* is the primary or the secondary element in the tradition, i.e., whether *alpha* is derived from *alphoi* or vice versa. Attempts to treat *alpha* as primary have proved unfruitful.[41] Instead, I am inclined to agree with I. Heinemann ("Moses," p. 361), who suggests that the designa-

---

[39] Both terms were in usage among pagan authors of the second century; cf. *hebraios* in Plutarch, *Quaest. conv.* 4.6.1, and *ioudaios*, in *ibid.* 4.5.2.

[40] The fact that each of the authors is presented as "uttering nonsense" (*phlyarein*) may also indicate that there was a common carrier of the tradition in Jewish or Christian apologetic circles.

[41] F. M. Th. Böhl, "Die Juden im Urteil der griechischen und römischen Schriftsteller," *Theologisch Tijdschrift* 48 (1914): 387, would derive *alpha* from the fact that Moses authored the first book of the Jewish scriptures. No pagan author refers to Moses in this manner, nor is it likely that *alpha* would have been used in any case. Böhl also suggests that the *alphoi* might be understood *in bonam partem*, as for instance the spots on Augustus' body which symbolized his power and divine origin. Even this, however, does not say that Augustus was a leper! Reinach, *Textes*, p. 122, n. 1, is at a loss to explain the origin of the tradition. He suggests that the first letter of the alphabet may have designated excellence among the ancient Jews. In a similar vein, I. Heinemann, "Moses," p. 361, suggests that *alpha* may also reflect the "monad" of Moses in the magical papyri (see below, pp. 146 ff.).

tion of Moses as *alpha* derives directly from the Alexandrian exodus tradition. Indeed the verbal similarities between Diod. Sic. 34.1.2 (*hoi gar echontes alphous ē lepras en tois sōmasi*) and Nicarchus (*dia to pollous echein alphous en tō sōmati*) are close enough to suggest that the account of Diodorus may have been the touchstone for the development of this tradition. Thus the understood subject of *kaleisthai* may be the grammarians themselves, i.e., "we call Moses *alpha* etc.*"* At the same time, this interpretation explains Helladius' mention of Philo as a witness in his favor. Philo nowhere calls Moses *alpha*, but in *Mos.* 1:79 he does report the miracle of Moses' leprous hand.[42] Thus Philo is not a witness for *alpha* but for the fact Moses did, if only for a brief moment, show signs of leprosy on his body.

If this interpretation is correct, the tradition is an example of onomastic-etymological puns, F. Dornseiff calls it a "Schulwitz,"[43] the purpose of which was to discover names of persons and places which could be related, by some clever means, to the letters of the alphabet. Such is the context in which Moses' name occurs in Helladius. One other figure in Helladius' text may shed light on the origin of the Moses saying. The mother of Cypselus, who was lame, was given the name Labda by the Pythian oracle. The pun here derives from the fact that one leg of the archaic letter *lambda* was shorter than the other and thus provided an alphabetic symbol of the limping Labda.[44] In these two cases the cognomen has arisen because of a similarity between an aspect of the person's bodily appearance and a letter of the alphabet. Apparently the correspondence *alpha-alphos* suggested itself to someone, probably a grammarian, who was familiar with the

[42] Exod. 4:6. Yahweh ordered Moses to put his hand in his bosom, and when Moses withdrew it the hand was "leprous, as white a snow." While the MT and the Samaritan text both explicitly say that the hand was leprous, Philo and the LXX report only that his hand was as white as snow. Other versions, however, read "leprous" (e.g., Aquila, Symmachus, and Theodotion). Whatever reading Helladius may have known in Philo, he clearly understood the passage to say that Moses' hand was leprous.

[43] *Das Alphabet in Mystik und Magie* (1922), p. 31. Further examples from the text of Ptolemy illustrate the technique. A certain Satyrus was called *zeta* because of his inquisitiveness (*dia to zētētikon autou*). A Roman military tribune, Galerius Crassus, was called *beta* because of his liking for a beet which was called *betaceum*. The origin of these sayings must have been like the origin of the saying about Moses, i.e., the alphabetical cognomen was derived from some known attribute of the person, not vice versa.

[44] The first occurence of the story of Labda is in Herodotus 5.921; cf. *Photius, Bibliotèque*, ed. R. Henry, 3 (1962) : 237 (note to p. 67).

widely known Alexandrian exodus tradition, thus giving rise to a tradition which survived to the time of Photius in the ninth century. Although the saying itself is based on Alexandrian material, we need not regard it as expressing an equal hostility toward the Jews. In its present form it is nothing more than a rhetorical exercise, a clever witticism.

Conclusion

Our survey of the figure of Moses in Alexandrian anti-Jewish literature has revealed the same motifs, cast in a different light and marshaled for quite different purposes, that we have earlier seen in Hecataeus of Abdera, Strabo, and Pompeius Trogus (above, pp 26 ff.). In contrast to the Alexandrian tradition, these pro-Jewish ethnographic accounts present Moses in a rather positive light. The accounts of Lysimachus, Chaeremon, and Apion, which were based on indigenous Egyptian legends, must have been formulated in conscious opposition to versions like those of Hecataeus, Strabo, and their Jewish counterparts. The basic structure of the story, including the central role of Moses, remains the same in both camps, but among the anti-Jewish writers Moses' virtues have turned into vices. No longer does Moses appear as a leader of superior theological wisdom. He is pictured rather as a rebellious and polluted Egyptian priest, expelled together with a mob of impure people, who later instituted a religious and social system motivated by an undying hatred of everything non-Jewish. As a weapon in the arsenal of anti-Jewish propaganda, this Alexandrian version of the exodus can no longer be regarded as conforming to the norms of Hellenistic ethnography.

Underlying the emergence of these anti-Jewish versions of the exodus tradition is a series of violent political and religious conflicts between Jews and foreign powers: the prolonged struggle between the Seleucid kings and the Maccabees in the second century B.C.E., the anti-Jewish riots at Alexandria in 39-40 C.E., and the Roman campaign against Judaea in 69-71. In each of these conflicts, political and religious factors were inextricably involved, and it is no accident that three of our authors, Manetho, Chaeremon, and Tacitus, were priests in the religious establishment of their respective people. For them, Moses' strange religious practices were no longer a matter of ethnographic curiosity but the root cause of violent religious and political confrontations which prompted equally violent political and literary countermeasures. Thus the representation of Moses as the symbol and the founder of a godless and hateful nation expresses not so much local chauvinism or xenophobia as it does the more or less official attitude which resulted from violent conflicts between Jews and non-Jews. Within the context of these conflicts, the accounts of Moses and the exodus served both to explain the bitter hostility of the Jews and to justify the repressive counteractions of the Seleucids, the Alexandrians, and the Romans.

4. Moses and Magic

Thus far in our study we have concentrated on the image of Moses among the lettered intelligentsia of Hellenistic and Roman imperial times—historians, grammarians, and the like. Our survey has shown a surprising amount of "information" and interest in Moses, together with two sharply divided schools of opinion. But Moses' renown, if we may call it that, was not limited to these literary figures. Beyond these learned circles, there is a body of evidence which indicates that Moses was equally, if not better, known within the more popular realm of magical theory and practice, although some of the strictly literary authors were not unaware of Moses the magician.[1] Pompeius Trogus (above, p. 49) speaks of Moses' *paterna scientia*, referring to his skill as an interpreter of dreams and prodigies, and Celsus (above, p. 95) proclaims that "the Jews worship angels and are addicted to sorcery of which Moses was their teacher." Others, including Numenius, are familiar with the contest of magic between Moses and Aaron and the court magicians of Pharaoh (below, pp. 137 ff.).

[1] On the reputation of the Jews as magicians, see Juvenal, *Sat.* 6.546 f.; Lucian, *Alex.* 32.13; cf. M. Simon, *Verus Israel* (1948; supplemented reprint, 1964), pp. 394-405.

Still, the bulk of the evidence is to be found among the documents of ancient magic and its half-sister alchemy, where Moses was a stock figure. Here we find more than ample evidence to support Celsus' claim that the Jews had learned the art of magic from Moses.

One basic problem confronts any attempt to evaluate references in magical documents not only to Moses but to the wide range of Jewish terms as well, including Adonai, Iao, Sabaoth, angelic names, and a host of magical names ending in -oth and -ath. The problem is of no little consequence because the number of documents with no Jewish elements at all is exceedingly small.[2] How, then, does one determine whether a magical papyrus or charm is of Jewish or pagan origin? E. R. Goodenough has established a sliding scale, beginning with charms in which Jewish elements predominate and which he calls Jewish, through charms where Jewish and pagan elements are so commingled that no clear decision is possible, to charms where Jewish elements are peripheral or totally absent.[3] Although even these pragmatic guidelines have failed to gain wide acceptance, Goodenough's basic thesis remains valid, i.e., it is no longer possible to regard every admixture of pagan and Jewish elements as the result of one-way borrowing by pagans from Jews.[4] On the other hand, H. Leon and A. D. Nock have accused Goodenough of erring in the opposite direction by showing himself too eager to accept items as Jewish merely because they include Jewish names.[5] "Once he

[2] So Goodenough, *Symbols*, 2:206, and C. Bonner, *Studies in Magical Amulets* (1950), p. 28.

[3] See the methodological discussion in *Symbols*, 2:153-55 and 206 f.

[4] See the discussion in M. Smith, "Goodenough's *Jewish Symbols* in Retrospect," JBL 86 (1967) : 67, additional note 2, *fin.* "The question of principle is now settled in Goodenough's favor by M. Margalioth's *Sefer ha-Razim* which demonstrates that magic of the type familiar from the Greek papyri was adopted and perpetuated by writers in the rabbinic tradition." See M. Margalioth, ed., *Sepher ha-Razim. A Newly Discovered Book of Magic from the Talmudic Period* [Hebrew] (1966). Margalioth tentatively dates the *Sepher* to the third century c.e. In 1896, M. Gaster in a study entitled the *Sword of Moses* (JRAS [1896], pp. 3-52; reprinted in his collected essays, *Studies and Texts* [1925-1928], 1:288-337) edited and translated a document of Jewish magical charms, written in Hebrew, to which he assigned a date in the first four centuries of the Christian era. Gaster believed that his text was of real significance for the study of Greek magical papyri and indicated that there was "much internal similarity between the Hebrew 'Sword' and the Greek papyri" (1:308).

[5] Leon, in his review of Goodenough in *Archaeology* 7 (1954) : 262; cf. Nock, in his review of Goodenough in *Gnomon* 27 (1955) : 570, where he agrees with

admits," says Leon, "that pagans commonly used Jewish names in their magic, the identification of purely Jewish ones becomes exceedingly dubious. . . ."

My own observation is that the distinction between Jewish and pagan in many cases presents a false alternative. The magical papyri and amulets reveal such a complex interpenetration of different religious vocabularies and ideas that traditional distinctions break down under the overwhelming weight of syncretism.[6] From the perspective of descriptive analysis it is often more accurate to speak of the Jewish or Greek contribution to a syncretistic document than to limit one's assessment of the document as a whole to Jewish or Greek. Speaking of PGM XIII, a typically syncretistic magical papyrus, Goodenough states that "Jewish elements are so mingled with pagan ones that I have no idea who could have written it."[7] To cite the case of Moses, the fact that he appears frequently in magical documents and alchemical treatises as a figure of great authority tells neither for nor against a Jewish origin of the documents as a whole. Properly speaking they are neither Jewish nor Greek nor Egyptian; they are syncretistic. Beyond this, certain individual terms like Iao, Adonai, Sabaoth, and Moses were so embedded in the vocabulary of syncretistic magic that they became permanent elements of the environment and thus were no longer strictly Jewish.

Finally, even if it should turn out that some of the individual charms are Jewish in origin, it remains true, as Goodenough has pointed out, "that all but three of the charms have been *preserved in collections made by pagans,* so that even those which seem exclusively Jewish, without any syncretistic features, clearly had value in pagan eyes" (*Symbols* 2:206). Thus as a practical solution, our examination of the charms, titles, and amulets will include all items which make mention of Moses, even though some of them may be Jewish in origin.

Goodenough's basic principle but states that he "probably goes too far." See also the excellent discussion in Bonner, *Amulets,* pp. 26-32.

[6] So Th. Hopfner, "Mageia," RE 27 (1928): 307, who states "[dass] schon vom 1. Jhdt. v. Chr. an kaum mehr von einer griechischen Religion u. von einem griechischen Z[auber] gesprochen werden kann, sondern nur noch von synkretistischer Theosophie und synkretistischer M[agie]. . . ."

[7] *Symbols,* 2:206, n. 229.

Moses, Jannes, and Jambres

Exod. 7:11-13 describes a contest between the magicians of Pharaoh and the magicians of Yahweh, Aaron and Moses, from which the Isrealite protagonists emerge victorious over their Egyptian adversaries. In subsequent times the story was retold and embellished in both Jewish and Christian circles. Not only did the Egyptians receive names (Jannes and Jambres or Mambres), but even their eventual conversion to Judaism was reported, apparently as a fittingly ironical climax to the legend.[8] On the Jewish side, the earliest reference appears in the Damascus Document (CD),[9] fragments of which have been discovered at Qumran,[10] which speaks of "Jannes (YḤNH) and his brother whom Belial raised up in the time of Moses and Aaron" (5.18 f.). On the Christian side, the earliest occurrence is 2 Tim. 3:8 which says simply that "Jannes and Jambres opposed Moses."

But knowledge of this legend was not limited to Jewish and Christian authors. In book 30 of his *Natural History*, Pliny the Elder (d. 79 c.e.) sketches a brief history of magic in which he lists a number of groups and individuals connected with the development of magic. Among them he includes a sect of the Jews: "There is another magical group, deriving from Moses, Jannes, Lotapes and the Jews, but many thousands of years after Zoroaster" (HN 30.2.11). Unlike the Damascus Document or 2 Timothy, Pliny shows no trace of the conflict between Moses and the Egyptians. On the contrary, Jannes is classified along with Moses, the unknown Lotapes, and the Jews as of common origin. If Pliny actually knew of a Jewish magical sect which claimed descent from Moses, Jannes, and Lotapes,[11] his statement is the only

---

[8] On the story in rabbinic and Christian tradition, see Schürer, 3:402-5; K. Koch, "Das Lamm, das Aegypten vernichtet, ein Fragment aus Jannes und Jambres," ZNW 57 (1966): 79-93; and esp. M. McNamara, *The New Testament and the Palestinian Targum to the Pentateuch* (1966), pp. 82-93.

[9] The original document, also known as the Zadokite Document, was discovered in the Cairo Genizah and first published by S. Schechter, *Documents of Jewish Sectaries* 1: *Fragments of a Zadokite Work* (1910; repr. with new prolegomenon by J. A. Fitzmyer, 1970).

[10] The fragments from Qumran were first published by M. Baillet, "Fragments du Document de Damas. Qumran, grotte 6," RBibl 63 (1956): 513-23, and finally in DJD, vol. 3: *Les "petites grottes" de Qumran*, ed. M. Baillet, J. T. Milik, and R. de Vaux (1962), p. 130; cf. the comments in McNamara, *Palestinian Targum*, p. 85, n. 31.

[11] Lotapes is unknown. Reinach, *Textes*, p. 282, n. 1, suggests that Lotapes refers to Jannes' companion, otherwise known as Jambres or Mambres. Other attempts to

testimony to its existence. More likely Pliny or his source, perhaps Apion, confused several distinct elements—Moses' reputation as a magician, the contest between Moses and Pharaoh's magicians, and the association of Moses' name with specific magical texts or groups—thus explaining Pliny's confused notice.[12]

A similar version of the legend is reflected in chapter 90 of Apuleius' *Apology:*

> If you find one trivial reason that might have led me to woo Pudentilla for the sake of some personal advantage, if you can prove that I have made the very slightest profit out of it, I am ready to be Carmendas, Damigeron, that Moses whom you know, Johannes, Apollobex, Dardanus himself or any other magician of note since the time of Zoroaster and Ostanes.[13]

At this point in the *Apology* Apuleius is about to refute the charge that he had married the widowed Pudentilla for purely financial reasons. His mention of the magicians, with whom he will gladly identify himself if proven guilty, is prompted by the additional charge that he had won Pudentilla's hand through the use of magic (*Apol.* 2).[14] The reference to Moses is noteworthy because it is introduced without any explanation. Either Apuleius knew that the name would be familiar to his audience, or, as is more likely, he wished to dazzle them with his erudition. In the immediately following paragraph (*Apol.* 91) he reveals that he had come across these names during his study *in bibliothecis publicis apud clarissimos scriptores.* Among

---

identify him have proven unsuccessful; cf. C. C. Torrey, "The Magic of 'Lotapes.'" *JBL* 68 (1949): 325-27, who attempts to show that it is a corruption of ΠΙΠΙ, a common Greek attempt to represent the Hebrew tetragrammaton.

[12] Just seven paragraphs later, in 30.6.18, Pliny mentions Apion "the grammarian" as one with whom he had conversed on the subject of magic.

[13] Carmendas is otherwise unknown; Damigeron appears in the list of magicians in Tertullian, *De Anima* 57; Apollobex (*Apollohaec* in the MSS) is called Apollobeches Coptites in Pliny, HN 30.2.9; Dardanus is known from the papyri as the author of magical texts; Ostanes, of Persian origin, enjoyed a considerable reputation as a magician and also "authored" magical writings. Moses' name is preceded by *his* in the MSS; it has been corrected most commonly to *is;* other proposals include *hic, iste, Hisus* (sc. Iesus), *Iudaeus,* and *Hebraeus.* On the corrections and the list of magicians, see A. Abt, *Die Apologie des Apuleius von Madaura und die antike Zauberei* (1908), pp. 318-25.

[14] On the legal basis of the charges relating to the use of magic, see Abt, *Apologie,* pp. 82-88, and R. MacMullen, *Enemies of the Roman Order* (1966), p. 324, n. 29.

these authors was probably Pliny the Elder. In view of the fact that six of the eight magicians mentioned by Apuleius (Moses, Johannes,[15] Apollobex, Dardanus, Zoroaster, and Hostanes) occur in Pliny, HN 30.2.8-11, this supposition seems likely.[16] As part of his preparation for the trial, Apuleius probably undertook research into the history of magic and in due course came across the list of magicians in Pliny, HN 30. On this assumption, Apuleius adds nothing to our knowledge of what pagan writers thought about Moses, except insofar as he confirms our basic contention that Moses' name was in circulation in Greek and Roman literary circles.

Finally, a rather different version of the story appears in the *On the Good* of Numenius:

> Next are Jannes and Jambres, Egyptian sacred scribes, men judged to be inferior to none in magic, when the Jews were expelled from Egypt. They were chosen by the people of Egypt to stand up to Mousaios, the leader of the Jews, and a man most powerful in prayer to god; and of the disasters which Mousaios brought upon Egypt they appeared able to turn away even the most violent (Fr. 18 Leemans).[17]

Numenius' account differs from those of his predecessors in several respects. He obviously knows more of the story than they. His description of Moses as "a man most powerful in prayer" marks him, as we have already seen, as well disposed toward Moses. The form of Moses' name (*Mousaios*) which Numenius uses occurs elsewhere in literary sources only in the Jewish apologist Artapanus, who claimed that the Greeks called Moses Mousaios when he reached manhood.[18] In Artapanus it obviously represents an attempt to identify Moses with Musaeus, the teacher of Orpheus, but it seems unlikely that Numenius had the same intention. In his case it is probably a simple adjustment of the orthography to the common Greek name. Another unusual feature of Numenius' version, which clearly differentiates it from its Jewish and Christian counterparts, is that Jannes and Jambres succeed

---

[15] The MSS read *ioh,* an abbreviation for *Iohannes* which is itself a variant form of *Iannes.* Thus there is no reason to correct the text to read Iannes, as most editors have done; cf. McNamara, *Palestinian Targum,* p. 87, n. 38.

[16] So Ganschinietz, "Iannes," RE 17 (1914) : 694.

[17] *Apud* Eusebius, *Praep. Evang.* 9.8.1-2 (411d) . Origen, *c. Cels.* 4.51, merely mentions that Numenius "narrates the story of Moses, Jannes, and Jambres."

[18] Artapanus *apud* Eusebius, *Praep. Evang.* 9.27.3 (432a) .

139

in turning away even the most violent of Moses' plagues. Here one is tempted to suppose that Numenius has consciously altered the story in order to deemphasize its pro-Jewish character.

If Pliny's information came to him from a pagan source, possibly Apion, Numenius' probably came from a written source. Such a writing did exist in Origen's time (d. *ca.* 254) and Numenius may well have been familiar with it some fifty years earlier.[19] At any rate, Numenius is the last pagan witness to the story. For Pliny, Apuleius, and Numenius the interest of the story probably lay in Moses' association with the world of magic. For us the story is of interest because it shows that already in the first century Moses was known among pagans as a magician.

Moses as an Intimate of God and Recipient of Divine Wisdom

Our main source of information concerning Moses as a magician is the corpus of magical papyri, the main bulk of which has been collected and edited by K. Preisendanz.[20] In addition there are a number of ancient texts related to the magical papyri, notably astrological and alchemical writings, where Moses is also present. Together they

---

[19] Origen, *Comm. in Matt.* 27:9 (ser. 117 *ad fin.*): ". . . 'as Jamnes and Mambres resisted Moses' is not found in the public writings, but in a secret book which is entitled, *Book of Jamnes and Mambres.*" Cf. also the title of an apocryphal book mentioned in the so-called Gelasian Decree, a Christian canon list of the sixth century, *Paenitentia Jamnis et Mambre.* Beyond this, M. R. James, "A Fragment of the 'Penitence of Jannes and Jambres,'" JTS 2 (1901): 572-77, has published a fragment from an eleventh-century manuscript, written in Latin and Anglo-Saxon, which he considers to be an excerpt from the *Penitence of Jannes and Jambres.* Koch, "Das Lamm," pp. 85 f., is willing to go even further and has proposed that the Latin text is based on an Aramaic original which he dates to pre-Christian times.

[20] *Papyri Magicae Graecae. Die griechischen Zauberpapyri,* ed. and trans. K. Preisendanz *et al.,* 1 (1928), 2 (1931). The projected third volume was never published, due to the destruction of the Teubner facilities during World War II. In 1964 Preisendanz, "Zur Ueberlieferung der griechischen Papyri," in *Miscellanea Critica,* ed. J. Irmscher *et al.,* 1 (1964): 203-17, published a list of the proposed contents of the third volume, together with other papyri published since 1931. He also noted that a microfilm of the page proofs for vol. 3 was in his possession (p. 217, n. 27). I have consulted a photographic copy of this volume, dated 1941, in the library of the Warburg Institute, University of London. Cf. also the list of magical papyri published since 1931 in R. Pack, *The Greek and Latin Literary Texts from Greco-Roman Egypt* (1965 ²), p. 2.

140

depict a Moses who enjoyed an intimate relationship with his God and who "authored" a series of magical and alchemical texts.

Moses, Adam, and Abel in Astrology

R. Reitzenstein has brought to light a most interesting reference to Moses in an astrological document, the Milanese Codex Ambrosianus E 16 sup. (= Catal. cod. astrol. graec. III: 32-40).[21] The text lists the thirty days of the month and to each day assigns the birth of a Greek deity, a biblical event, and a series of activities which are regarded as appropriate or inappropriate for the given day. Thus on the second day Phosphoros was born, Eve was created from Adam's side, and the day is favorable for those who wish to wed. On four of the thirty days, however, there is no mention of a Greek deity but instead an allusion to the Jewish scriptures: on the first day Adam, ho prōtoplastos, was born; on the fourth day Abel; on the nineteenth day Moses; and on the twenty-ninth day the Jews entered the promised land.

There are a number of possible explanations, none of them entirely satisfactory, of the four exceptions to the normal order of the list. Obviously the present text represents an amalgamation of Greek and Jewish traditions, of which the Jewish is probably prior to the Greek.[22] One possible explanation of its anomalous character is that a non-Jewish interpolator introduced the Greek elements into the Jewish original and regarded the four items as sufficiently well known to warrant being left unchanged. While this might account for Adam, Moses, and the occupation of the promised land by the Jews, it is difficult to imagine that Abel would also fall into the same category. Another possibility is that the interpolator in question was himself a Hellenistic Jew. This would account for the four exceptions and at the same time disqualify the text as a pagan witness to Moses. In view of this second possibility, we should probably regard the text as contributing little to our particular concern for what pagans knew and thought about Moses.

[21] Poimandres (1904), pp. 271 f. The date of the text is uncertain. The manuscript dates from the thirteenth century, and Reitzenstein calls it a "hellenistische Ueberarbeitung," but the "hellenistisch" seems to apply to the content of the text rather than to its date.

[22] Reitzenstein, Poimandres, p. 271, refers to a similar and purely Jewish list in Paris. graec. 2316, fol. 331 and Codex Antinori 101, fol. 242, which begins with Adam and concludes with Samuel, just as in our Greco-Jewish list.

Moses Receives the Revelation of the Great Name

In the biblical narrative Moses communicated directly with Yahweh on two special occasions, once on Mount Horeb where Yahweh revealed his name to Moses (Exod. 3:1–4:31) and once again on Mount Sinai where Moses received the divine law (Exod. 19 ff.). The revelation of the divine name, the tetragrammaton, was the starting point in Judaism of a widely held superstition concerning the power of the name. Both Philo (*Mos.* 2.114) and Josephus (*AJ* 2.276) refused to speak or write it. Such was the power of the name that Pharaoh, according to Artapanus, fell as if dead when Moses whispered the divine name in his ear, and a priest who made light of the name which Moses had written on tablets died of convulsions.[23] Thus to know this particular divine name was to dispose of considerable magical power. In this sense the greatest contributions of Judaism to the syncretistic world of magic were the divine names which appear so frequently in the papyri: Iao, Sabaoth, Adonai. The fact of this Jewish contribution is evident, and it is interesting to note that it is attributed explicitly to Moses at several points in the papyri.

The first instance is a syncretistic charm in PGM V, lines 108-18, in which Moses proclaims,

I am Moses, your prophet, to whom you committed your mysteries which are celebrated by Istrael; you showed forth moisture and aridity and every kind of nourishment. Listen to me! I am the messenger of Phapro Osoronnophris. This is your authentic name which was committed to the prophets of Istrael.[24]

The charm itself is dedicated to "Osiris the headless," invoked as Osoronnophris "the good Osiris"):[25]

I call you the headless one, who created earth and heaven, who created night and day, you who created light and darkness. You are Osoronnophris,

---

[23] *Apud* Eusebius, *Praep. Evang.* 9.27.25 f. (435a). On beliefs about the magical power of the divine name, see L. Blau, *Das altjüdische Zauberwesen* (1914 ²), pp. 117-46; G. F. Moore, *Judaism* 1 (1927): 423-29; and J. Trachtenberg, *Jewish Magic and Superstition* (1961), pp. 78-103. See also Origen's discussion in *c. Cels.* 5.45 ff.

[24] For discussions of PGM V, and esp. of lines 99-171, see A. Dieterich, *Abraxas* (1891); Reitzenstein, *Poimandres*, pp. 184-86; E. Norden, *Agnostos Theos* (1913), pp. 187 f.; K. Preisendanz, *Akephalos: Der kopflose Gott* (1926), pp. 42-44; and Goodenough, *Symbols*, 2:197.

[25] On Osoronnophris as a name of Osiris, see Preisendanz, *Akephalos*, p. 43.

whom no one has ever seen, you are Iabas, you are Iapos,[26] you distinguished right from wrong, you made female and male, you pointed out seed and fruits, you made men to love and to hate one another (lines 98-108).

Here the influence of the account of creation in Gen. 1 is obvious.[27] As for Moses, the prophet and guardian of Yahweh's revealed mysteries, it should be recalled that both Philo (*Mos.* 1.57,156) and Josephus (*AJ* 4.329) knew Moses as a prophet and that both likened the Mosaic religion to *mysteria*.[28] Although the papyrus does not specify the content of the *mysteria*, the "authentic name which was committed to the prophets of Istrael" must have been an important element. Thus it would appear that Moses has been singled out in this thoroughly syncretistic charm for having made known to the initiates the authentic divine name which is here invoked for magical purposes. A similar connection between Moses and the revelation of the great name appears in several other papyri. PGM II, lines 126-28 read,

I am him who met you, and you gave to me as a gift the knowledge of your greatest name. . . .[29]

PGM III, lines 158 f. read,

[26] The forms *Iabas* and *Iapos* are probably variants of Iao; see the discussion in Blau, *Zauberwesen*, pp. 131 f.

[27] "Heaven and earth" in Gen. 1:8-10; "night and day" in Gen. 1:5; "light and darkness" in Gen. 1:4; "male and female" in Gen. 1:27; and "seed and fruits" in Gen. 1:11. A. Abt, "Nucularum hexas," *Philologus* 69 (1910): 141 ff. has also called attention to echoes of Exod. 17:1-7; 14:15, 21; 16:1 ff. in lines 108 ff.

[28] Philo, in *Cher.* 49, says, "and I have been initiated into the greater mysteries by the god-beloved Moses." In *Ap.* 2.189 Josephus chides the Greeks because "practices which under the name of mysteries and rites of initiation other nations are unable to observe for but a few days, we maintain with delight and unflinching determination all our lives." On mystery language in Hellenistic Jewish literature generally, see Goodenough, *By Light, Light* (1935).

[29] Line 114 of the same papyrus (P. Berlin 5026) reads *epi gēs eismouseōs ephanēs tē alētheia*. A. Abt in PGM vol. 1, p. 28 note *ad loc.*, reads the problematic phrase as *eis Mouseos* ("im Hause des M."), while the printed text has *epi gēs e<r>ismous theos gar ephanēs* . . . (". . . for you have truly appeared as god . . ."). The textual problem is discussed by Preisendanz, "Ein Pseudo-Moses," ArchRW 19 (1916-19): 195 f. He concludes that the scribe failed to understand the text of his master copy, *epi gē seismou*, and read it instead as a reference to Moses. Other elements of Jewish origin in the papyrus include Sabaoth and Adonai (lines 115 ff.); the charm itself is dedicated to Apollo.

I am him whom you encountered and to whom you granted knowledge of your greatest name and of its sacred pronunciation. . . .[30]

Finally, PGM XII, lines 92-94 read,

I am him whom you encountered under/at the foot of the sacred mountain, and you granted knowledge of your greatest name, which I will keep and transmit to no one except to fellow initiates in your sacred mysteries.

Although none of these formulaic statements mentions Moses by name, Preisendanz and others have identified the speaker as Moses.[31] This identification is suggested not only by the similarity to PGM V, lines 108 ff., where Moses is named, but by other texts both within and without the magical papyri. It will be recalled that the full title of PGM XIII is the *Eighth Book of Moses concerning the Holy Name* and that a similar title, *Secret Book of Moses concerning the Great Name,* appears in lines 731 f. Outside the papyri, a passage from Josephus' *Antiquities* (2.275 f.) presents the same picture:

Moses, unable to doubt the promises of the deity, after having seen and heard such confirmation of them, prayed and entreated that he might be vouchsafed this power in Egypt; he also besought Him *not to deny him the knowledge of His name,* but . . . to tell him how He should be addressed, so that when sacrificing he might invoke Him by name to be present at the sacred rites. Moreover, Moses found those miracles at his service not on that occasion only but at all times whensoever he was in need of them. . . .

Here the relationship between the revelation of the divine name and the performance of miracles through it is patently clear. Taken together, these various pieces of evidence indicate that the "great name" and its revelation among men appears in the magical papyri in association with Moses.

Moses in the Demotic Magical Papyrus of London and Leiden
Another testimony to the prominent role of Moses in the magical papyri is a Demotic magical papyrus edited by F. L. Griffith and

[30] In line 444 of the same papyrus Moses' name appears together with Abraxas, Iao, and Sabaoth. The text is broken at this point, and it is not possible to determine the context of the reference.
[31] Preisendanz, "Laminetta Magica Siciliana," *Acme* 1 (1948) : 77, n. 2, and Reitzenstein, *Poimandres,* p. 293, n. 1.

H. Thompson.[32] In this Egyptian document dating from the third century C.E., Moses appears twice as an ideal type of one who enjoys an intimate relationship with the gods. In the first passage, the speaker implores the god,

reveal thyself to me here today in the fashion of thy revelation to Moses (*mwes*) which thou didst make upon the mountain, before whom thou didst create darkness and light.[33]

The second passage is part of a love charm in which the speaker requests the gods to awaken a longing between a man and a woman like the longing of God for Moses,

the longing which the god, the son of Sopd (?), felt for Moses going to the hill of Ninaretos to offer water to his god, his lord, his Yaho, Sabaho, his Glemura-muse, Plerube . . . S Mi Abrasaz, Senklai . . . (verso, col. 12, lines 6-8).

Assuming that the text has been read and translated accurately, the passage presents a number of puzzles. Presumably Glemura-muse, Plerube, S Mi Abrasaz, Senklai are magical names such as normally follow the invocation of the deity. The phrase "the god, the son of Sopd (?) " is peculiar in that the god longs for Moses, not Moses for the god. The hill is probably a reflection of the fact that Moses met Yahweh on a mountain, but the name Ninaretos is unknown. As for the water-offering, no such incident is connected with Moses in the biblical account.[34] Water was commonly used in rites of purification, but apparently not in sacrifice proper before the exile. In the Hellenistic period, however, a libation of water was introduced into the

[32] *The Demotic Magical Papyrus of London and Leiden* (1904); see the discussion of introductory problems, pp. 1-18. The papyrus is written in a mixture of Hieratic and Demotic, with frequent Coptic glosses, and consists mainly of formulas designed to bring about visions of the gods; other material includes recipes for love potions, poisons, and assorted drugs. On non-Egyptian influence the editors say the following: "The influence of purely Greek mythology also is here by comparison very slight—hardly greater than that of the Alexandrian Judaism which supplies a number of names of Hellenistic form . . ." (v).

[33] Col. 5, lines 13 f. The "darkness and light" is related to the brilliant light normally associated with theophanies; see the discussion in T. Hopfner, *Griechisch-Aegyptische Offenbarungszauber* 2 (1924): 102-114.

[34] See 2 Sam. 23:16, where David, rather than drink water procured for him at great risk, pours it out as a kind of offering to Yahweh.

145

feast of tabernacles.[35] The rabbis justified this innovation by claiming that Moses had received it as part of his revelation on Mount Sinai. In terms of its function within the love charm, the mention of Moses again establishes him as one who enjoyed a special relationship with the deity, so much so that the longing of the god for Moses could be likened to the love which the charm sought to create between a given man and woman.

Magical Charms and Writings Attributed to Moses

The Eighth Book of Moses

Holy Book called the Monad or the Eighth Book of Moses concerning the Sacred Name (Biblos hiera epikaloumenē Monas ē Ogdoē Moyseōs peri tou onomatos tou hagiou). Such is the title in line 3 of the Leiden Papyrus J395 (= PGM XIII), dating from the third or fourth century c.e.[36] Actually the title applies only to the first half of the papyrus. The papyrus as a whole comprises two recensions of the same text (A=1-233 and B=343-734), each encompassing magical charms of all kinds and an account of creation inserted in the midst of the charms (A=139-206 and B=443-565).[37] Appended to each recension is a mixed bag of magical names and charms (234-342 and 735-1078). The title of B (345) is Secret Holy Book of Moses, called the Eighth or Sacred (Moyseōs hiera bi<b>los apokryphos epikaloumenē Ogdoē ē Hagia). At the end of A (341) the author refers to the writing simply as the Holy and Blessed Book, Monas, while B (724-734) presents three different, though related, titles. The first appears between two vertical lists of names used to calculate the presiding

---

[35] On the feast and the water libation, see G. F. Moore, Judaism 2 (1927): 44-46. The details for the ceremony are discussed in Mishnah Sukkoth 4.9. The Talmudic justification appears in b.Suk.34a: "They had this as an accepted tradition; for R. Assi (ca. 300 c.e.) said in the name of R. Jonathan (fl. ca. 250 c.e.), 'The ten plants, the willow branch and the water libation were given to Moses upon Mount Sinai.'"

[36] For a description of the papyrus and relevant bibliography, see K. Preisendanz in ArchP 8 (1927): 122 f. The text is also published in Dieterich, Abraxas, pp. 165-205. His description of the contents of the papyrus (pp. 154-66) is the most complete known to me.

[37] On the possibility that the cosmogony reflects the Genesis creation story (LXX), see PGM 2:87, n. 1; 95, nn. 1-2; 110, n. 1, and the references therein to the unpublished paper of A. Jacoby, "Zur Entstehungsgeschichte der Leidener Kosmopoiie."

planet on any given day: *Monad of Moses,* also called *Commentary, Heptazonos.* Two more follow the lists and appear to be colophons—"*Secret Eighth Book of Moses;* in another copy which I found was written, *Secret Book of Moses concerning the Great Name*" etc.[38]

To summarize, of the several occurrences of the title in the two recensions Moses' name appears in five (lines 3, 345 f., 726, 731, 732 f.) and in each case the title is different. In three of the five (3, 345 f., 726) the titles are compounds of two or more elements, e.g., "*Secret Holy Book of Moses,* called the *Eighth* or *Sacred.*" The variation in the form and content of the titles demands some clarification. One possibility is that several different writings or titles have been combined into one on the basis of common authorship. A. Dieterich proposed this solution for the two titles in lines 731-733, suggesting that the *Secret Book of Moses concerning the Great Name* should not be identified with the *Secret Eighth Book of Moses.*[39] A second possibility is that the titles *Monad* and *Eighth Book of Moses* were created for the purpose of attaching greater prestige to the document which may have had nothing to do with Moses in its original form.[40] A third explanation is that titles and material of Jewish origin have been absorbed by the syncretistic milieu and worked into the magical papyri themselves.[41] The fact that the Pentateuch was known in Hellenistic

---

[38] The possibility that *heptazonos* belongs to the list rather than to the title itself must be held open as a possibility. The actual text reads as follows:

ἐὰν γὰρ ἡμέρα Ἡλίου εἰς τὸ Ἑλ⟨λ⟩ηνικόν, | Σελήνη πολεύει. οὕτως καὶ οἱ ὕστεροι, οἶον.

Ἑλληνικόν·		ἑπτάζωνος·
Ἥλιος	Μοϋσέως Μονας,	Κρόνος
Σελήνη	ἡ καὶ ὑπόμνημα	Ζεύς
Ἄρης	ἐπικαλουμένη,	Ἄρης
Ἑρμῆς	ἑπτάζωνος	Ἥλιος
Ζεύς		Ἀφροδίτη
Ἀφροδίτη		Ἑρμῆς
Κρόνος		Σελήνη

Μοϋσέως ἀπόκρυφος η'. ἐν ἄλλῳ, ⟨ὃ⟩ | εὗρον, ἐγέγραπτο· | Ἡ Μοϋσέως ἀπόκρυφος βίβλος περὶ τοῦ μεγάλου | ὀνόματος, ἡ κατὰ πάντων, ἐν ᾗ ἐστιν τὸ ὄνομα τοῦ διοικοῦν⟨τος⟩ | τὰ πάντα.'

[39] *Abraxas,* p. 155.

[40] So Bonner, *Amulets,* p. 27.

[41] Other elements of Jewish origin in the papyrus include Iao, Adonai, Sabaoth, and occasional angel names; there are also two references to Jerusalem, one in line 996 ("the great name in Jerusalem") and one in lines 233 f. ("As I made you swear in/by [en] the temple in Jerusalem . . .") .

Judaism as the Five Books of Moses lends further credence to the idea that at least the *Eighth Book of Moses* is of Jewish origin.[42] *Monas* is the first of three titles shared by Moses and Hermes; the fourth tractate of the *Corpus Hermeticum* is entitled *Ho Kratēr ē Monas.*

A Supposed Tenth Book of Moses

In the last line (1077) of PGM XIII are written the words *Moysēos apokryphos ē/hē* followed by one word apparently written in abbreviated form.[43] This final word was first read by C. J. C. Reuvens in 1830 as *dekatē,* a reading which has been accepted with only occasional hesitation in subsequent editions.[44] Based on this reading, the words have been interpreted as referring to another writing, the *Secret Tenth Book of Moses.* There are, however, several other possible interpretations which warrant consideration. If the *ē* is read as a conjunction ("or"), there is a parallel in lines 344 f.: *Moysēos biblos apokryphos . . . Ogdoē ē Hagia.* If the *ē* is read as the feminine article *hē,* i.e., *Moysēos apokryphos, hē dekatē,* there is no parallel in the papyrus. The problem with both these interpretations is that a tenth book is nowhere else attested, nor is there any reference to the ninth book which one might have expected between the eighth and tenth. If, on the other hand, we forget temporarily the uncertain letters which have been read as *dekatē* and read the *ē* as the numeral eight (8), we have *Moysēs apokryphos ē,* i.e., *Secret Eighth Book of Moses,* for which there is an exact parallel in line 731, the colophon to the main section of B (see above, n. 38). Finally, even if we accept *dekatē* as the correct reading, there is a strong possibility that its presence is the result of a scribal error or a gloss of some sort.[45]

[42] There is no evidence for the existence of a sixth and seventh book of Moses. Dieterich, *Abraxas,* p. 160, n. 3, notes that in modern times ambitious persons, exploiting the absence of these intervening books, have run advertisements in European newspapers announcing the availability of "Magical books, Sixth and Seventh Books of Moses."

[43] So PGM XIII, note to line 1077.

[44] Reuvens, *Lettres à M. Letronne* (1830), p. 152; so also Dieterich, *Abraxas,* p. 205, who admits that he was not able "die ganz flüchtigen Buchstaben sicher zu lesen"; and PGM 2:131 (note to line 1077).

[45] Reuvens, *Lettres,* p. 152, notes that the line over the *ēta* designates a number, not an article. Although he regards his reading of the ligature as correct, he attributes it to a scribal error and suggests that the original text was meant to read, *Eighth Secret Book of Moses:* ". . . je serais tenté de croire que le copiste ou le reviseur, dont l'ignorance est visible dans toutes les pages, en prononçant la lettre numérique *ēta* . . . comme *iota* s'est trompé également dans sa valeur."

The Key of Moses

A second title, the *Key* (*Kleis*) *of Moses,* also appears in **PGM** XIII. It is cited four times in A (22, 31, 36, 60) and three in B (383, 431, 737); of these, 36 is parallel to 383 and 60 to 431. The attribution to Moses occurs once in each recension. In each instance the writer refers to a book where the reader will find certain information. Line 22 contains a quotation from the *Key:* "Over everything keep ready some sun-vetch" (*orobon hēliakon*). The injunction belongs to the preparatory stages of the initiation into the cult of the Monad, around which the main section of the text is constructed. From line 383 we learn that the writing also included the names of "the hour gods and the day gods and the formula by which they are constrained. For he himself [*sc.* Moses] drew them down" (*autos gar autous apespasen*). In other words, the efficacy of the formula is guaranteed because Moses himself used it with success. Finally, line 738 adds that the eight-letter name which is great and wonderful is also recorded in the *Key.* From these few indications it is hardly possible to reconstruct the work as a whole. As noted, in their present setting they belong to the preparatory stages of the rites of the Monad, whose ultimate goal is a revelation from the Monad himself.

Like *Monad, Key* is also found as part of a title among the Hermetic writings. The tenth tractate of the *Corpus Hermeticum* is called the *Key of Hermes Trismegistus.* The fact that these two terms appear as book titles here and in the Hermetic writings indicates something like a rivalry between Moses and Hermes.[46] Further evidence of the competition is line 14 of our papyrus where the writer charges that "Hermes stole from this book [*sc.* the *Eighth Book of Moses*] when he named the seven sacrificial fumes in his holy book, the *Wing.*" On the Jewish side, the rivalry appears most sharply in the apologetic Moses romance of Artapanus where Moses performs the feats normally attributed to Hermes-Thot and is dubbed Hermes by the grateful Egyptian priests (see above, p. 77).

The Archangelical Book of Moses

A third book is attributed to Moses in PGM XIII, lines 971 f.: "According to Moses in the *Archangelical Book* . . ." (*en tē Archange-*

---

[46] So Dieterich, *Abraxas,* p. 165; Festugière, *Révélation,* 1:288; and E. Peterson, "Das Amulett von Acre," in *Frühkirche, Judentum und Gnosis* (1959), p. 353.

likē . . .). The title appears as one among a list of writings from various figures, including the *Parastichis* of Orpheus (934), a writing of Zoroaster the title of which is lacking (967) and "the Law written in Hebrew" (976). Following each title is a series of magical words supposedly quoted from the work. Thus the quotation from Moses' *Archangelikē* begins " *'Aldazao batham machōr'* or *'Baadammachōr rizzaē ōkeōn pned meōy.* . . .' "

R. Reitzenstein claimed to have found further remains from Moses' *Archangelikē* in a manuscript of the fifteenth century. The passage in question reads as follows:[47]

> Phylactery of the servant of god (name), for the protection and guarding of your servant (name): *archangelical hymn* which God gave to Moses on Mount Sinai. . . .

In its present form the phylactery is clearly Christian, but behind it Reitzenstein posits a Jewish document which reaches back to at least the second century C.E.

With the discovery and gradual publication of the Coptic documents from Nag Hammadi further light has been shed on our book. A writing without title from codex 2 of the Nag Hammadi texts mentions an *Archangelikē* of Moses:

> You will find the influence (*energeia*) of these names and the power (*dynamis*) of the masculine in the *Archangelikē* of the prophet Moses (150. 7-9).[48]

There seems little doubt that this book and the one cited in PGM XIII, lines 971 ff. are somehow related. The Coptic text is a translation from Greek and probably dates from the early fourth century,[49] the same date assigned by the editor to PGM XIII. Furthermore, the names whose power is said to be described in the *Archangelikē* of Moses are listed just before our passage (149.28-32) and include *Iaō, Sabaōth,* and *Adōnaios*—i.e., precisely those names which occur so frequently in the magical papyri. Whether the two writings are actually identical and whether Reitzenstein's text is also related to them cannot be demonstrated one way or the other. But the fact that the

[47] *Poimandres,* pp. 292 f.
[48] *Die koptisch-gnostische Schrift ohne Titel aus Codex II von Nag Hammadi,* ed. and tr. A. Böhlig and P. Labib (1962), pp. 46 f.
[49] See the paleographic discussion of Nag Hammadi Codex 2 in S. Giversen, *Apocryphon Johannis* (1963), pp. 34-40.

gnostic as well as the magical writing quote an *Archangelikē* of Moses indicates that the writing or writings must have been in fairly wide circulation and must have enjoyed a considerable reputation in the syncretistic circles of Egypt.

The Secret Moon Book of Moses

Yet a fourth title appears in line 1057 of PGM XIII as part of the extended appendix to recension B: *"Secret Moon Book of Moses"* (*Moysēs apokryphos Selēniakē*). The title is followed by five lines of magical words and an appeal to the moon goddess: "O goddess in female form, empress Moon, fulfill such and such a deed." [50]

It is uncertain whether our title applies only to the few lines of material cited in PGM XIII or whether there existed a more substantial work. A clue may be provided by PGM VII, line 862, which refers to a "book" the title of which begins *Klaudianou Selēniakon*. In the subsequent context a *logos selēniakos* is cited (line 879) which appears to designate only the petition (or "ode," see line 889) which follows in lines 880-889 and is there introduced with the words, "I call upon you, queen of the whole cosmos." Although the evidence from PGM VII is not unambiguous, it suggests that Moses' *Secret Moon Book* may have contained more than the single prayer recorded in PGM XIII.

The Diadem of Moses

A final title, the *Diadem of Moses,* appears in PGM VII where an excerpt is quoted in lines 620-628.[51] The papyrus is a random collection of magical charms. The charm from Moses' *Diadem* promises success in making the user invisible, in securing the love of a woman, and generally in fulfilling any desire:

From the *Diadem of Moses,* "Take a kynokephalidion plant, place it under your tongue when you lie down to sleep; in the morning, before you speak, pronounce the names and you will be invisible to all. And when you speak over a drinking cup and give it to a woman she will love you, as this charm

[50] Reitzenstein, *Poimandres*, p. 190, cites a late Latin manuscript in which a book with a similar title is attributed to Hermes: "Hermes Agathodaemon, father of philosophers, most ancient wise man and, as it were, one of the philosophers blessed by god, published a *Book of the Moon* (*librum Lunae edidit*)."

[51] For a description of the papyrus (British Museum P. Greek 121), see PGM 2:1.

works in every case [Magical words, including *Iaō*, *Sabaōth* and *Adōnai*]. For whatever you desire say, 'Do such and such to so and so!' Anything you want."

The origin of the charm is uncertain. Although it names no non-Jewish figures, the only Jewish elements are *Iaō, Sabaōth, Adōnai*, and Moses, none of which is strong evidence of immediate Jewish influence. In any event, like all the titles and charms discussed above, it has been removed from its original setting and integrated into a typically syncretistic collection of magical formulas.

Alchemical Writings Attributed to Moses

Closely related to the development of magic, yet distinct from it, is the emergence of alchemy or *hē theia kai hiera technē,* as it was commonly known among its advocates.[52] As among ancient practitioners of magic, so also among alchemists Moses enjoyed a considerable reputation. His name occurs in the first position in a list of "Names of philosophers of the divine wisdom and art," where he appears along with Democritus, Xenocrates, Heraclitus, and Zosimus as one of the great men in the history of alchemy.[53] In the *Oath* (*horkos*) of Pappas the philosopher, Pappas quotes an alchemical recipe from Stephanus, a seventh-century alchemist, and states that the same recipe appears in his own writing *To Moses the Thrice-Blessed* (*Pros Moysea ton triseumoiron*).[54] To a somewhat greater extent than among magicians, Moses was forced to share his reputation as an alchemist with other Jewish figures, notably Maria the Jewess and Solomon.[55] Maria in particular seems to have been an important

---

[52] On the origins of alchemy, see E. Riess, "Alchemie," RE 2 (1894): 1338-55; W. Gundel, "Alchemie," RAC 1 (1950): 239-60 and the literature there cited; and J. Lindsay, *The Origins of Alchemy in Graeco-Roman Egypt* (1970). The pioneering work of M. Berthelot, *Les origines de l'alchimie* (1885), represents the first serious effort to lay bare the origins and early history of alchemy. The only edition of the ancient texts, *Collection des anciens alchimistes grecs,* edited by Berthelot and C.-E. Ruelle, 1 (1887), 2-3 (1888), is regarded by Gundel ("Alchemie," pp. 239 f.) as uncritical and unreliable. See also the series *Catalogue des manuscrits alchimiques grecs,* published by the Union Académique Internationale (1924-   ).

[53] Berthelot-Ruelle, 1 (Introduction): 110 f.

[54] *Ibid.,* 2:28 (text), and 3:30 (trans.).

[55] On Maria the Jewess, see Berthelot, *Origines,* pp. 56, 171-73, and Gundel, "Alchemie," pp. 241 and 245. On Solomon, see Gundel, p. 246 and Loren R. Fisher, " 'Can This Be the Son of David?' " in *Jesus and the Historian,* ed. F. T. Trotter (1968), pp. 82-97. Little is known of Maria apart from the writings quoted by

figure for Zosimus, a third-century alchemist, who quotes frequently from her works. At the same time and probably in the same circles, a number of alchemical treatises were in circulation under Moses' name.

The Diplōsis of Moses

A *Diplōsis* or recipe for producing gold from baser metals, is ascribed to Moses in the Saint Mark manuscript, which dates from the eleventh century.[56] A similar title, *Peri Diplōseōs Chrysou*, is attributed to Moses in a list, perhaps a table of contents, at the head of the same manuscript.[57] The two are probably variants of the same title. Concerning the date of the recipe, Berthelot and Gundel concur in setting it near the time of Zosimus.[58] The recipe reads as follows:

Copper of *kalainos,* one ounce; arsenic and native sulphur, one ounce; virgin sulphur, one ounce; red sulphide of arsenic, one ounce. Emulsify with radish oil and lead for three days. Put in a dish and place on the fire until it desulphates; remove and you will find what you wish. This is one part copper and three parts gold. Melt while narrowing the funnel and you will find, with the help of god, the whole to be gold.

The Chemistry of Moses

The Paris manuscript 2327, dating from 1478, contains a writing entitled the *Chemistry of Moses*.[59] The approximately twenty pages include items on the treatment of mercury, pyrite, and arsenic and the production of gold and various kinds of copper. The discourse opens with a paraphrase of Exod. 31:2-5, which is clearly designed to demonstrate the antiquity and respectability of alchemy:

And the Lord said to Moses, "I have chosen the priest, Beseleel by name, of the tribe of Judah, to work gold, silver, copper, iron, all workable stones and wooden artifacts, and he will be a master of all trades."

Zosimus. Gundel, p. 245, mentions an Arabic MS in Cairo which bears her name and claims to be translated from Greek; it deals with various metallurgical formulas.

[56] On the date of the manuscript, see Berthelot, *Origines*, p. 97. The text appears in Berthelot-Ruelle, 2:38 f. (see 3:40).

[57] *Ibid.,* 1:175 (no. 37).

[58] *Ibid.,* 1:202; Gundel, "Alchemie," pp. 245 and 249.

[59] Berthelot-Ruelle, 2:300-315 (text), and 3:287-302 (trans.). It should be noted that the title appears only in the French translation and not in the printed Greek text.

The date of the formula is unknown. Berthelot notes that several of the recipes occur also in the second-century writings of Pseudo-Democritus, and uses this as evidence, albeit rather weak, for an early dating of the *Chemistry* as a whole.[60]

According to Berthelot there is a further reference to the *Chemistry* in a treatise entitled *Poiēsis Krystalliōn.* In discussing methods of lending deeper color to tinted stones, the author refers to a formula in the *Private Chemistry of Moses:* "Concerning which the divine (*thespesios*) prophet Moses speaks in his *Private Treatise on Chemistry.*" [61] The designation of Moses as "the divine prophet" again raises the question of Jewish influence, although there is nothing else in the treatise which would require or even suggest it. Inasmuch as the term "prophet" was one of the many designations applied to alchemists, not even this need indicate Jewish influence.[62]

The Maza of Moses

In his treatise on the *Standard of Yellow Dyeing* Zosimus twice refers to a *Maza* of Moses, a metallurgical work dealing with methods of treating various stones and metals.[63] The first reference is introduced in support of a particular method of firing metals:

Everyone burns in this way. *The Maza of Moses:* "Burn as follows, with sulphur, salt and alum (I mean white sulphur)." [64]

The second reference also concerns techniques of firing:

[60] Berthelot-Ruelle, 3:287, n. 7. On the date of Pseudo-Democritus, see the discussion in Festugière, *Révélation*, 1:222ff.

[61] Berthelot-Ruelle, 2:353 (text), and 3:338 (trans.): *en tē oikeia chymeutikē taxei.*

[62] According to Zosimus, Democritus wrote to the "Egyptian prophets" on the wonders of alchemy (Berthelot-Ruelle, 2:159); a certain Chimes, quoted by Zosimus, was known as a prophet (*ibid.,* 2:183); and a writing attributed to "the Christian" mentions a female alchemist whom it calls "the Hebrew prophetess" (*ibid.,* 2:404).

[63] The term *maza* can be used to designate a lump of metal, as of gold (Josephus, *AJ* 5.33); in the alchemical papyrus (P. Leiden 10, ed. C. Leemans, p. 2), the term appears as the title of a recipe for the preparation of a lump of metal. The *Maza of Moses* should probably be understood as a title much like the one in P. Leiden 10. For a discussion of the term *maza* in later authors, see Berthelot-Ruelle, 1 (Introduction): 209 f. and 257.

[64] Berthelot-Ruelle, 2:182 (text), and 3:180 (trans.).

And in the *Maza of Moses*, near the end, the following is written: "Pour water on virgin sulphur and it will become yellow and shadowless." [65]

These references are especially important because they enable us to place the *Maza* in or before the time of Zosimus (third cent. C.E.). Furthermore, it is on the basis of this certain dating that Berthelot has assigned an early date to the *Diplōsis*, the *Chemistry*, and the *Private Chemistry*. Whether or not the evidence of the *Maza* can be thus applied to other writings, it does attest the existence, no later than the third century, of at least one pseudonymous alchemical writing of Moses which was cited as an authority by Zosimus and later alchemists.

Once again we are faced with the question of the possible Jewish origin of the writings in question. Some of the titles themselves, especially those of Maria the Jewess, would seem to indicate that there existed a school of Jewish alchemy in the early centuries of the Christian era.[66] On the other hand, as with the magical charms, the titles and the excerpts from the writings have been preserved in non-Jewish circles. Thus there is no way of determining with certainty whether the titles represent Jewish traditions or whether they were invented by non-Jews using the well-known name of Moses as a pseudonym. This much is certain; the two realms of magic and alchemy reflect in different ways the syncretistic environment of second, third, and fourth-century Egypt, and in this world the name of Moses carried considerable authority.[67]

Amulets and Phylacteries

Two Moses Amulets

In his collection of magical amulets, C. Bonner has drawn attention to two stones which bear the name of Moses. One is described as "showing a snake between the words *Sabao* and *Iao*, with *Moysē* on

[65] Berthelot-Ruelle, 2:183 (text), and 3:181 (trans.).

[66] Apart from these names and titles there is no other evidence of Jewish alchemy in the early centuries of the Christian era; see the discussion by R. Eisler, "Zur Terminologie der jüdischen Alchemie," MGWJ 69 (1925): 364-71, and "Zur Terminologie und Geschichte der jüdischen Alchemie," MGWJ 70 (1926): 194-201.

[67] This affinity is further indicated in that PGM XIII (the *Eighth Book of Moses*) and two alchemical papyri (P. Leiden 10 and P. graec. Holm.) were discovered in the same tomb at Thebes and were copied by the same hand; see the discussion in Festugière, *Révélation*, 1:221, nn.3-4.

the reverse." [68] On such amulets the figure of the snake normally represents the Egyptian deity Chnoubis, a healing god,[69] but Goodenough notes that it might also represent the bronze snake made by Moses in Num. 21:9; "I suspect," he continues, "that the amulet would never have been made had it not been designed by a Jew who wanted protection from intestinal disorders which, as he had learned from his neighbors, the figure of a snake on an amulet would bring." Goodenough concludes that "only the most rigorous double standard would regard this as anything other than a probably Jewish amulet." [70] Goodenough's "probably" needs to be emphasized. *Iaō* and *Sabaōth* were in wide circulation in magical circles and even the name of Moses had become almost common property. Thus if the snake represents Chnoubis, which Goodenough accepts as probable, we must admit that the probability of Jewish origin is somewhat reduced.

Bonner describes the second amulet as follows: "Obv[erse]. Mummy (not characterized as Osiris) to front, feet to r[ight]. Curious gablelike headdress, face indistinct. At l[eft], αβραξας, at r[ight], Μωσην, below, ζοζζοζ Rev[erse]. σενσενγενβαρανγης, in four lines." [71]

In interpreting this stone Goodenough has amalgamated the inscribed names and figures from this and the preceding Moses-Iao-Sabao amulet and thus arrives at the following description: "Moses is the snake is the mummy is Osiris is Iao in a sort of Gertrude Stein confusion." [72] Here again Goodenough's view may require certain modifications. The presence of Moses' name indicates nothing more than that it was widely regarded as a powerful magical name, nor is there much more reason to assume than to deny the identification of Moses, Abraxas, and the mummy. Rather than identifying them we might perhaps consider them as an effort to invoke three different powers

---

[68] *Studies in Magical Amulets*, p. 171; cf. the discussion in Goodenough, *Symbols*, 2:266-67.

[69] On Chnoubis' amulets in general, see Bonner, pp. 25 f. and 54-60, and Goodenough, *Symbols*, 2:261-69.

[70] *Symbols*, 2:266.

[71] *Amulets*, p. 255 (no. 13). The term *se (n) sengenbar (phar) angēs* occurs frequently in magical texts; cf. Hopfner, *Offenbarungszauber*, 1 (1922) : 191. Josephus, *BJ* 7.178-185 describes a plant with power to kill anyone who touches it but also to expel demons, which grew in the ravine (*pharangos*) near a place called *baaras*. Hopfner suggests that the magical term is probably related to some combination of these two words, *baaras* and *pharanges*.

[72] *Symbols*, 2:267.

for the certain fulfillment of the amulet's intended purpose.[73] Given the frequency with which the names *Abraxas* and Moses occur in magical documents there is no way of determining with certainty who produced or used them. The owner may have been a Jew, but he may just as well not have been.[74]

A Moses Phylactery[75]

Moses' name appears in the last line of a silver phylactery which was discovered rolled up in a bronze case at a grave site in Amisus (Pontus). The sheet measures 6.7x4.5 cm. and contains an inscription of 20 lines. It has been discussed by S. Petrides and R. Wünsch, both of whom have published facsimiles of the item, but there is no photograph against which to check their numerous divergent readings.[76]

[73] Normally names on amulets belong to the figures they accompany, e.g., Chnoubis. Nevertheless, there are enough exceptions to the rule to require caution in its application.

[74] Another amulet that has been connected with Moses is described by A. Delatte and P. Derchain, *Les initiales magiques gréco-égyptiennes* (1964), pp. 312 f. (no. 455) as follows: "In the center is an extremely gross and altered representation of a coiled snake who seems to be the bronze serpent given by Moses to the Hebrews. To its left, on a base line, six figures are advancing toward the snake. The first figure is holding a palm branch. M. Barb suggests that they are Israelites in search of healing. Above them are two lines of characters. To the right of the snake, Moses, with raised arms and a halo over his head, is crouched near a tree and a sort of comb which apparently represents the flame of the burning bush. Above him an angel is descending head first from heaven. Near the angel's feet is a large star and below it are four inscribed characters. The number of these characters, the presence of two I's and their position close to the star might suggest a corruption of the word πιπι, a frequent transcription of the tetragrammaton Yahweh in Greek magical texts. . . . In subject and style, the stone is already Byzantine." In addition, the stone shows a large letter *M*, not mentioned in the description. Prof. Morton Smith has suggested to me that the letter is actually the monogram −M−, very likely for *Mē (tēr theou)* "mother of God") ; see also Smith's review of Delatte and Derchain in AJA 71 (1967) : 417-19. In any case, the amulet is probably Byzantine and therefore beyond the scope of our immediate concern.

[75] Cf. also a Moses phylactery from Sicily, almost certainly Jewish, published by A. Vogliano, with commentary by K. Preisendanz, "Laminetta Magica Siciliana," *Acme* 1 (1948) : 73-85; and the discussion of the phylactery by E. Peterson, "Das Amulett von Acre," in his collected essays, *Frühkirche, Judentum und Gnosis* (1959), pp. 346-54.

[76] See Petrides, "Amulette judéo-grecque," *Echos d'Orient* 8 (1905) : 88-90 (Petrides' text is reproduced in CIJ, no. 802, together with additional comments by J.-B. Frey) ; Wünsch, "Diesidaimoniaka," ArchRW 12 (1909) : 24-32, with a drawing

The final sentence, "I am he who holds reign over[77] the place in the name of Moses," is perplexing. The speaker, in this case the deceased Rouphina, raises the claim that the *topos* is protected by the deity in the name or through the agency of Moses.[78] The expression "in the name of Moses" is unique, but the underlying idea of an intimate relationship between Moses and his god is quite in harmony with the image of Moses throughout the magical papyri and amulets.

Once again the question of possible Jewish origin arises. The occurrence of the name Rouphina in a Jewish inscription from Smyrna indicates that it was in use among Jews,[79] but it was also a common Roman proper name. As for the origin of the divine and magical names, Wünsch and Petrides agree that the text contains an equal

---

of the text and extensive commentary. The respective transcriptions compare as follows:

Petrides	*Wünsch*
'Εγώ εἰμι ὁ μέγας ὁ ἐν οὐ-	(same)
ρανῷ καθήμενος,	(same)
τὸ μολόν αὖγος ὅλου	τὸ μολὸν κύτος ὅλου
τοῦ κόσμο (υ) . "Αρσενος ΒΡΕ	τοῦ κόσμο (υ) 'Αρσενο[νεο-
5 Φρὴ σάον ὄνομά μ (ο) ι 'Αρ-	φρις σαον ὄνομα Μιαρ-
σὰ (φ) ὡς δ (α) ίμων ἀ (γ) α-	σαυ ως δ (αί) μων αλα-
θός. βαριχαάκ, μηφίβ.	θος βαριχαα Κμῆφι ὁ
βασιλέων τῶν βασιλέ-	βασιλε (ύ) ων τῶν βασιλ (ε) ι-
ων. ἀβριαώθ. ἀλαρφρώθ,	ῶν 'Αβριαὼθ 'Αλαρφώθ
10 οισήθ. θοῶν μηκέτι	οι Σήθ θεων· μηκέτι
κακὸν φ (αι) νέσθω. ἀπέλα-	(same)
σον, ἀπέλασον ἀπὸ 'Ρου-	(same)
φίνην τὴν ὑπόθεσιν.	φίνης τὴν ὑπόθεσιν·
καὶ εἴ τίς με ἀδικήσ (η) ἀπεκ (ε) ινα,	καὶ εἴ τίς με ἀδικήσ (ει) , ἐπ' ἐκ (εῖ) νον
15 ἀπόστρεψον. μήτε δε φάρ-	ἀπόστρεψον· μήτε με φάρ-
μακον ἀδικήσ (η) . βασιλέα	(same)
βασιλέων. ναρβιαώ, ἱπώ,	βασιλέων 'Αβριάων τω
ὀρθιαρή. 'Εγώ εἰμι ὁ βαστά-	Ορθιαρη· ἐγώ εἰμι ὁ βασιλί-
ζων τὸν τόπον, εἰς ὀνόμα-	(same)
20 τι Μ (ω) ϋσ (ῆ) .	τι Μοϋσ (ῆ) .

[77] So Wünsch; Petrides reads "upholds" or "supports."

[78] Wünsch, "Deisidaimoniaka," p. 31, interprets the occurrence of *eis* with the dative as an error resulting from an omission, and proposes *eis (ton aiōna en) onomati* as the original text. A simpler explanation might be scribal ignorance. Wünsch (p. 31) also remarks that *topos* is used in an unusual manner. The term normally designates the place in which a magical act takes place. He suggests that it has been clumsily transferred in our text to refer to the phylactery itself and thus to the owner. Frey's attempt (CIJ 2:54) to explain *topos* as a translation of *maqōm*, a common rabbinic circumlocution for Yahweh, fails because *topos* here is quite distinct from the god and refers to something over which he rules.

[79] CIJ, no. 741, dating from the third century c.e. or later; on Rouphina, see the literature there cited.

number of Egyptian and Jewish terms. As Egyptian, Wünsch designates *Arseno[neo]phris* in lines 4 f. as a Greek form of the Egyptian divine name Osornophris;[80] *Kmēphi* in line 7 as a form of Chnum;[81] and *Seth* in line 10 as the Egyptian deity Seth. As Jewish he cites *Abriaoth* and *Alarphot* in line 9 and *Abriaon* in line 17.[82] Thus far the evidence is inconclusive. The only remaining piece of evidence is Moses in line 20, which Petrides regards as decisively favoring a Jewish origin. But on the basis of our survey of magical documents, even this cannot be accepted as conclusive. It is no less likely that a non-Jewish phylactery should refer to Moses as the spokesman or agent of the god in question than a syncretistic document like the *Eighth Book of Moses* should be attributed as a whole to him. At the same time, the possibility that Rouphina was Jewish should not be excluded.

Conclusions

In assessing the image and role of Moses in these documents, the first observation is that he is nowhere called the lawgiver of the Jews.[83] In this respect the Moses of the magical and alchemical documents is largely independent of the Moses in the Greek and Roman literary tradition, although some of the literary authors were familiar with Moses' reputation as a magician. The almost casual manner in which Celsus and Apuleius seem to assume his reputation indicates two important facts: first, the image of Moses as magician was not limited to Egypt, and, second, it was already well established in the second century C.E., while the even earlier comment by Pliny pushes the date back to the middle of the first century. The significance of these chance remarks among literary authors is that they enable us to date some of the material in the papyri, most of which are from the third

[80] On *Arsenophrē* and related forms, see Hopfner, *Offenbarungszauber*, 1:189. Wünsch (p. 25) notes that the letters *NEO* at the end of line 4 seem to be a correction written over the letters *ZM*.

[81] On *Kmēphi* and other similar forms, see Wünsch, "Deisidaimoniaka," p. 28 and the literature there cited. Plutarch, *De Is. et Os.* 359D, says that the residents of Thebes honor a god whom they call *Knēph*.

[82] "Deisidaimoniaka," pp. 27-29. On the many forms of *Abriaoth* in magical texts, see Ganschinietz, "Iao," RE 17 (1914) : 703 f.

[83] It should be noted, however, that PGM V, lines 108 f. ("I am Moses . . . to whom you revealed your mysteries") may refer to the law as a mystery.

and fourth centuries, considerably earlier than the documents themselves.

On the whole, however, the Moses of the magical documents is a figure unto himself. Here he emerges as an inspired prophet, endowed with divine wisdom and power, whose very name guaranteed the efficacy of magical charms and provided protection against the hostile forces of the cosmos. To what did he owe this exalted status? The magical papyri themselves provide at least a partial answer. Jewish tradition and Egyptian syncretism agreed that Moses possessed a higher knowledge of the divine than most mortals. For advocates of the magical arts, whether Jewish or not, the essence of this revealed *gnosis* was Moses' knowledge and transmission of the divine name, not the tenets of the law as in the Jewish scriptures and much of rabbinic Judaism, nor his knowledge of the future as in some circles of Jewish apocalypticism. The revelation of the divine name to Moses was also regarded as an important event within Judaism, and because of its immediate relevance for magic this particular event was commemorated in the papyri more often and more emphatically than any other events associated with the life of Moses. In this regard, we must presuppose, as Goodenough, Nock, and others have suggested, the direct and active participation of Jews in the syncretistic milieu which produced the magical documents.[84]

Together with his role as the revealer of the divine name and the prophet of God, Moses was also considered to be the "author" of magical books and charms, as well as of alchemical treatises. That his role as an author is related to, perhaps even dependent on, his function as a prophet seems certain, although the connection is nowhere made explicit. There is little direct evidence within the Judaism of our period that Moses was regarded as the author of magical or alchemical books. The Hebrew *Sword of Moses* (see above, p. 135, n. 4) certainly falls into this category, but its late date prevents us from using it as an archetype of writings like the *Maza*, the *Diadem*, or the *Eighth Book of Moses*. As for Jewish alchemy, there is little independent evidence for its existence in this period. The main evidence consists of the pseudo-Mosaic writings themselves, from

---

[84] On the significance of the *Sepher ha-Razim* as a witness to the mutual influence of Jewish and pagan magic, see the work of Margalioth, above, p. 135, n. 4.

which we can only guess that books of magic and achemy may also have been attributed to Moses within Judaism.

But influence from what we know of ancient Judaism does not, as we have said, account fully for the position of Moses in these ancient documents. Like Iaō, Abraxas, and a host of magical terms of Hebrew origin, Moses seems to have enjoyed something of an autonomous existence in the tradition; like them he was no longer strictly Jewish.[85] Probably in the magical papyri and almost certainly in alchemical circles, the name of Moses was attached to individual charms and recipes precisely because it had come to represent considerable authority within these groups. But it is inexplicable that this should have happened unless there had been important traditions and practices involving Moses which impressed magicians and alchemists. Whatever these traditions and practices were, they must be located in a form of Judaism rather different from that reflected in most of the preserved evidence—a Judaism whose syncretistic tendencies prepared the groundwork for the later assimilation of Moses by magicians and alchemists in Egypt.

[85] K. Preisendanz, "Laminetta Magica," p. 77, remarks that Moses' name was "[ein] unentbehrliches Requisit des Zaubermarkts."

Conclusion

Our initial observation is that pagan authors of Hellenistic and Roman imperial times knew more about Moses than one might commonly expect. It is probably fair to say that few authors in this period knew nothing about him and that most knew at least his name. Beyond this, the amount and quality of information varied considerably, ranging from garbled bits of rumor to firsthand familiarity with biblical and other Jewish writings. At the same time we should note that with the exception of the "magical" documents, our evidence comes from the lettered elite. What, if any, knowledge of Moses existed outside these rather limited circles is altogether unknown.

If we ask why Moses captured the attention of the pagan world to the almost complete exclusion of other Jewish figures, the answer must be twofold. One obvious reason is that he was already established as the hero *par excellence* within Judaism of the post-exilic period. This is evident not only in the writings of Artapanus, Philo, and Josephus, but quite generally in all aspects of post-exilic Jewish literature. Thus the prominence of Moses in pagan writers is in large part a reflection of his prominence in Judaism itself. A second reason is that once he had become established in pagan eyes as the representative of Judaism, his position was further enhanced by virtue of his particular role as the lawgiver of the Jews. From the perspective of pagan historiography and ethnography, this role marked him immediately as the key figure of Jewish history.

The three basic images of Moses in pagan writings—the lawgiver, the leader of the exodus, and the practitioner of magic—correspond in the main to the same categories within Judaism. Initially, the basic information pertaining to these images came from Jewish sources. In the pre-Christian era, these sources were broadly speaking apologetic, i.e., designed to cast Moses in a role acceptable to Jews and pagans according to the standards of a common Hellenistic culture. In the first two Christian centuries, these sources were often transmitted by Christian writers, e.g., by Justin to Celsus, by Origen to Porphyry, and by Eusebius to Julian. A final stage was reached some time after 150 c.e. when the Jewish scriptures also became known directly to pagan writers (Celsus, Porphyry, and Julian), who used them to supplement and often to modify other sources of information. In each case, however, this basic information was supplemented with material supplied by the pagan authors themselves. Hecataeus of Abdera and Strabo embellished their information with motifs from Greek philosophical and religious traditions; Pseudo-Manetho and Apion amalgamated certain basic facts about the exodus with indigenous Egyptian stories of despised foreign invaders; and the writers of magical texts affixed Moses' name to charms and books of every kind and origin. These are, so to speak, the literary or internal factors responsible for what the pagan world knew of Moses.

The first and most enduring reaction of the Greek world to Moses was positive. Even at times when the Jews as a people were despised and reviled on all sides, Moses' status as a wise lawgiver persisted. The familiar pattern of ideal beginnings and later degeneration served to isolate him, in Strabo, Tacitus, and Julian, from criticisms normally directed against the Jews. But this pattern did not prevail in every case. Especially in Alexandria, but also under the Seleucids and later in Rome, the influence of external factors, political and religious, caused Moses not to be distinguished from his people but rather to be held fully responsible for the very worst of their sins.[1] In the end,

---

[1] The most complete and satisfactory account, to my mind, of the political and religious factors in ancient anti-Semitism, better anti-Judaism, is to be found in Tcherikover, *Hellenistic Civilization*, pp. 368-77. He dismisses the economic

however, the more positive view of Moses prevailed. In the second and third Christian centuries he was still a significant and authoritative figure for Numenius and Porphyry, while in Egypt, the home of his most bitter detractors, his status as a powerful magician was exalted and durable.

---

factor altogether. Instead he sees the roots of the conflict, which he prefers to call a misunderstanding, in the ambiguous civic status of the Jews in the diaspora. They enjoyed the privileges of the cities but shared in none of the political responsibilities and rejected outright their gods. Tcherikover (p. 375) cites as evidence Apion's statement, "If the Jews are citizens, why do they not worship the same gods as the Alexandrians?" (Josephus, *Ap.* 2.65.)

Index of Biblical Passages

165

Index of Persons and Subjects

167